Mandala Heaven

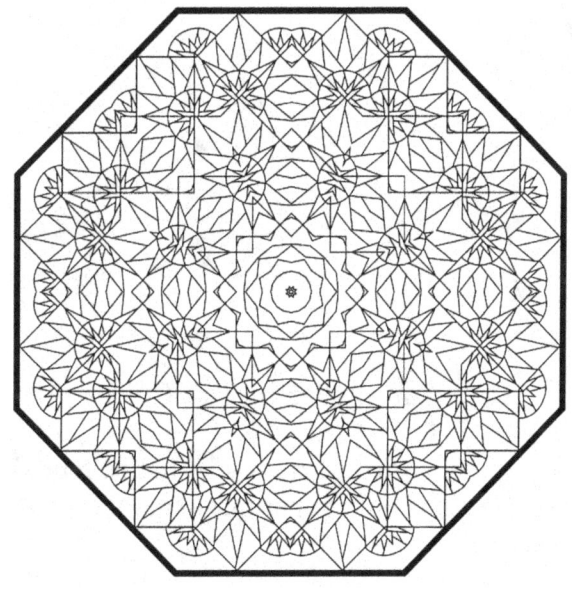

Volume Three: 35 Intricate Designs
For Your Coloring Pleasure

Designs by Tina Golden

Printed in the United States of America

First Printing, 2015

ISBN-13: 978-1519586988
ISBN-10: 1519586981

Tina Golden
Doodletime Designs
16 Maple Street
Augusta, ME 04330

http://www.DoodletimeDesigns.com

Welcome to Mandala Heaven Volume Three!

Let me start by saying there is no wrong way to color. It is supposed to be fun, creative, and relaxing. It's not very relaxing to have negative thoughts or get anxious over how your picture is turning out. Take a deep breath, let go of any negativity, and just be in the moment while you color these designs.

Coloring is a great way to release your inner creativity. A lot of people find that coloring inspires them to be creative in other areas of their lives, so when you're feeling stuck about something – color!

I recommend colored pencils or other dry media with this book, but you can use other media such as gel pens or markers if you take some care. Wet media can bleed through the pages onto another design. To avoid that, make sure to put an extra sheet of paper or card-stock behind the page you're coloring. There are two extra blank sheets at the back of the book that you can use for this purpose if you don't have card-stock handy.

If there is an image that you really want to turn out a certain way, feel free to photocopy the image onto the paper of your choice. I find a light-weight card stock perfect for my own coloring. It holds up nicely to markers and gel pens, but has enough tooth to work great with colored pencils, as well.

Photocopying your favorite designs can really allow you to relax and go with the flow when coloring as it takes all the worry out of it. It's an automatic do-over because you still have the original to print another. It's also a great way to try a different color palette.

I enjoy seeing how other people color my designs and learning about their techniques, so I'd love to have you share any finished pieces on my Facebook page or tag me on any social media channels we're both on. And both authors and artists thrive on reviews so please help me out by posting a review on Amazon – your support will enable me to keep bringing you new and exciting coloring books.

See you there!

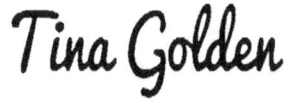

Connect with me

Facebook: https://www.facebook.com/DoodletimeOriginals
Twitter: https://twitter.com/ArtByTinaGolden
Pinterest: https://www.pinterest.com/tmgenterprises/

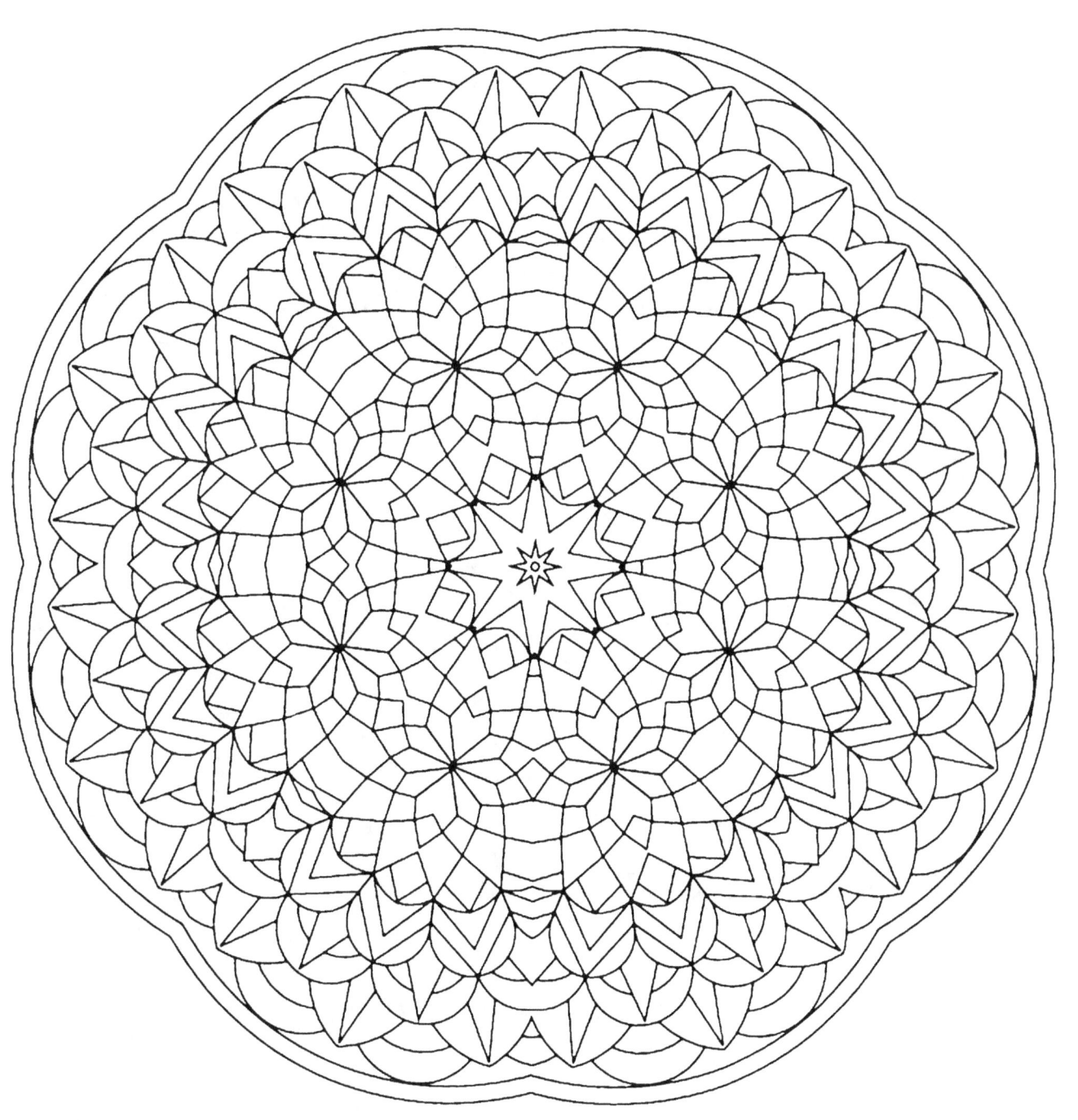

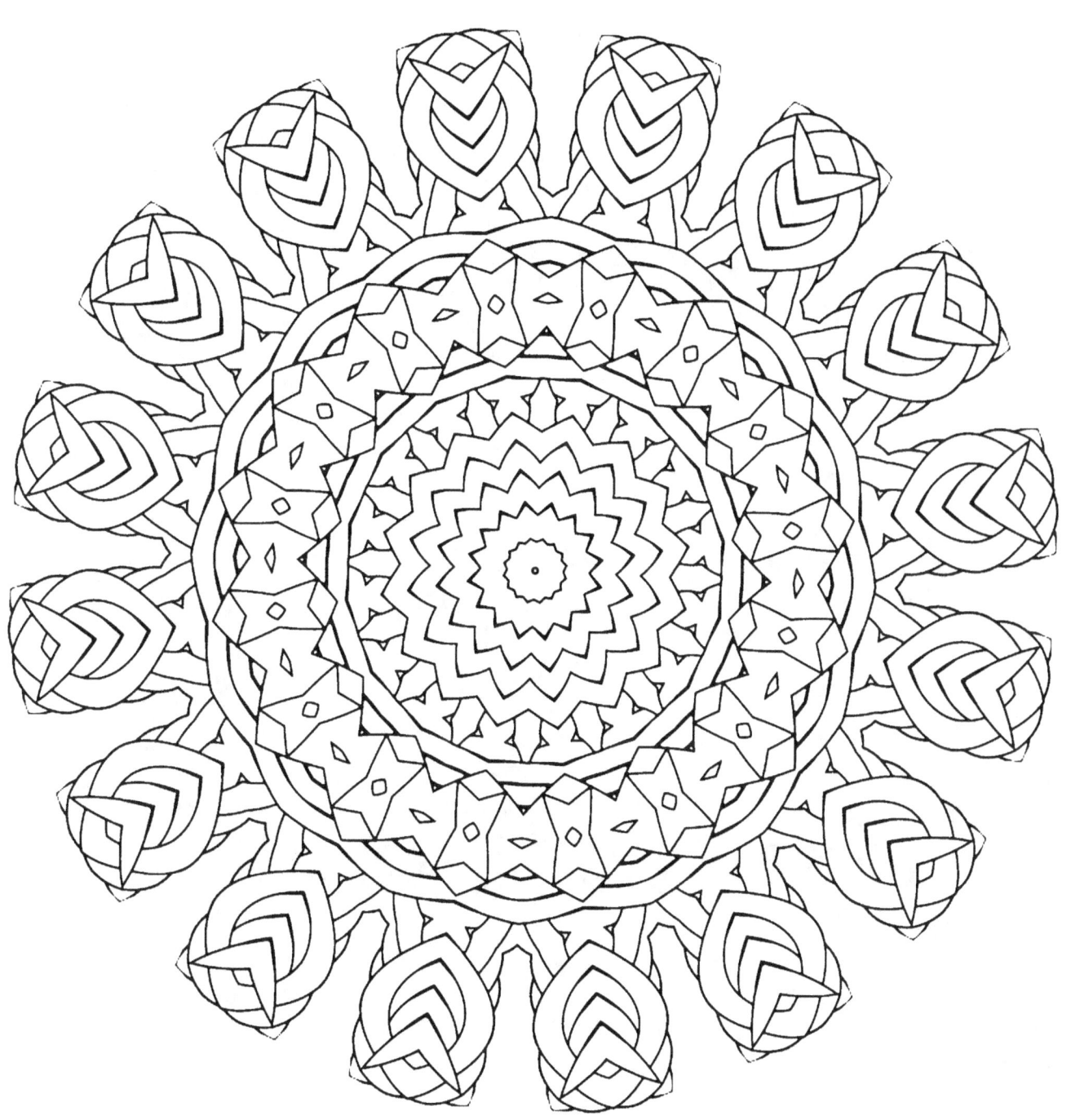

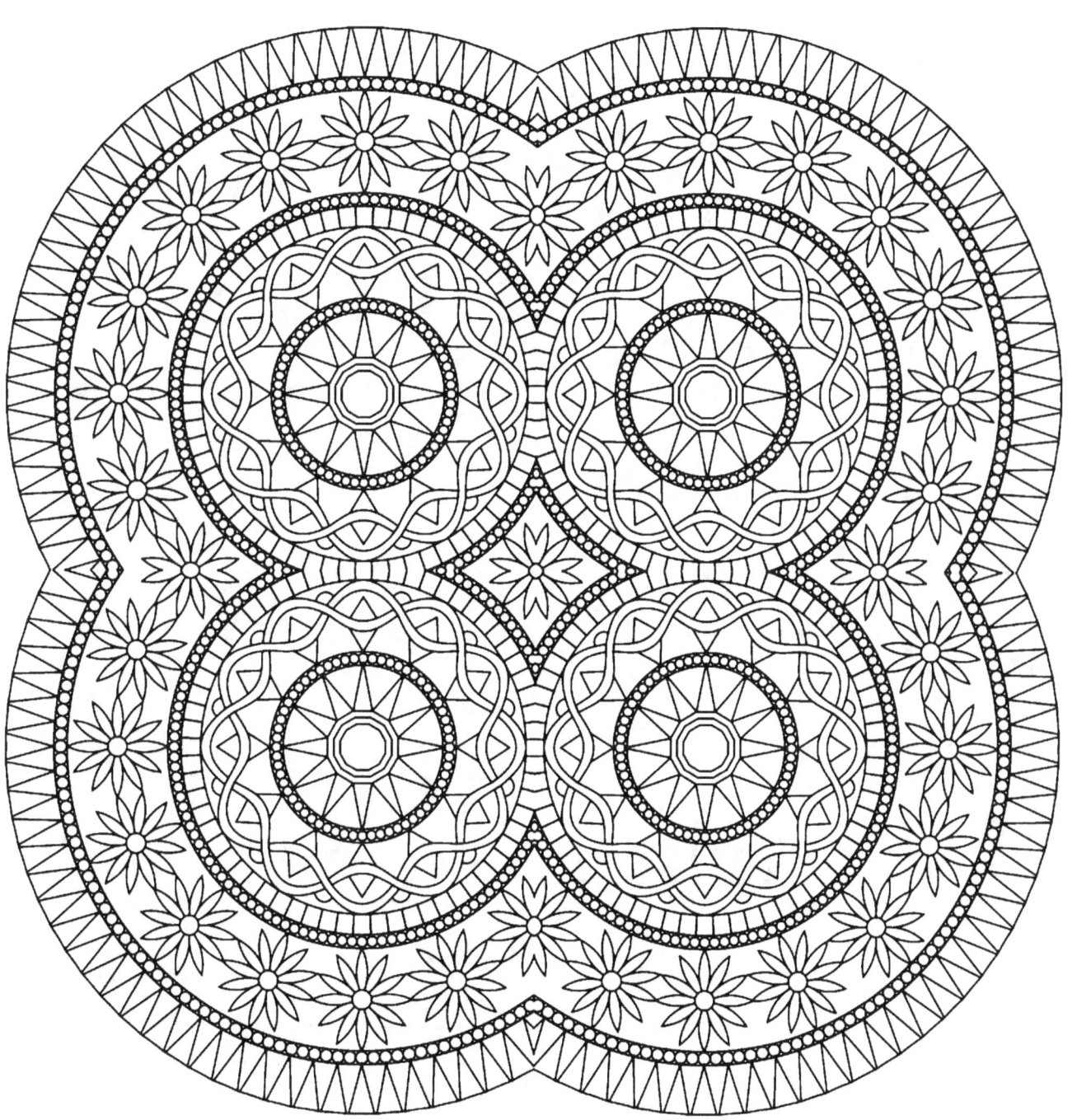

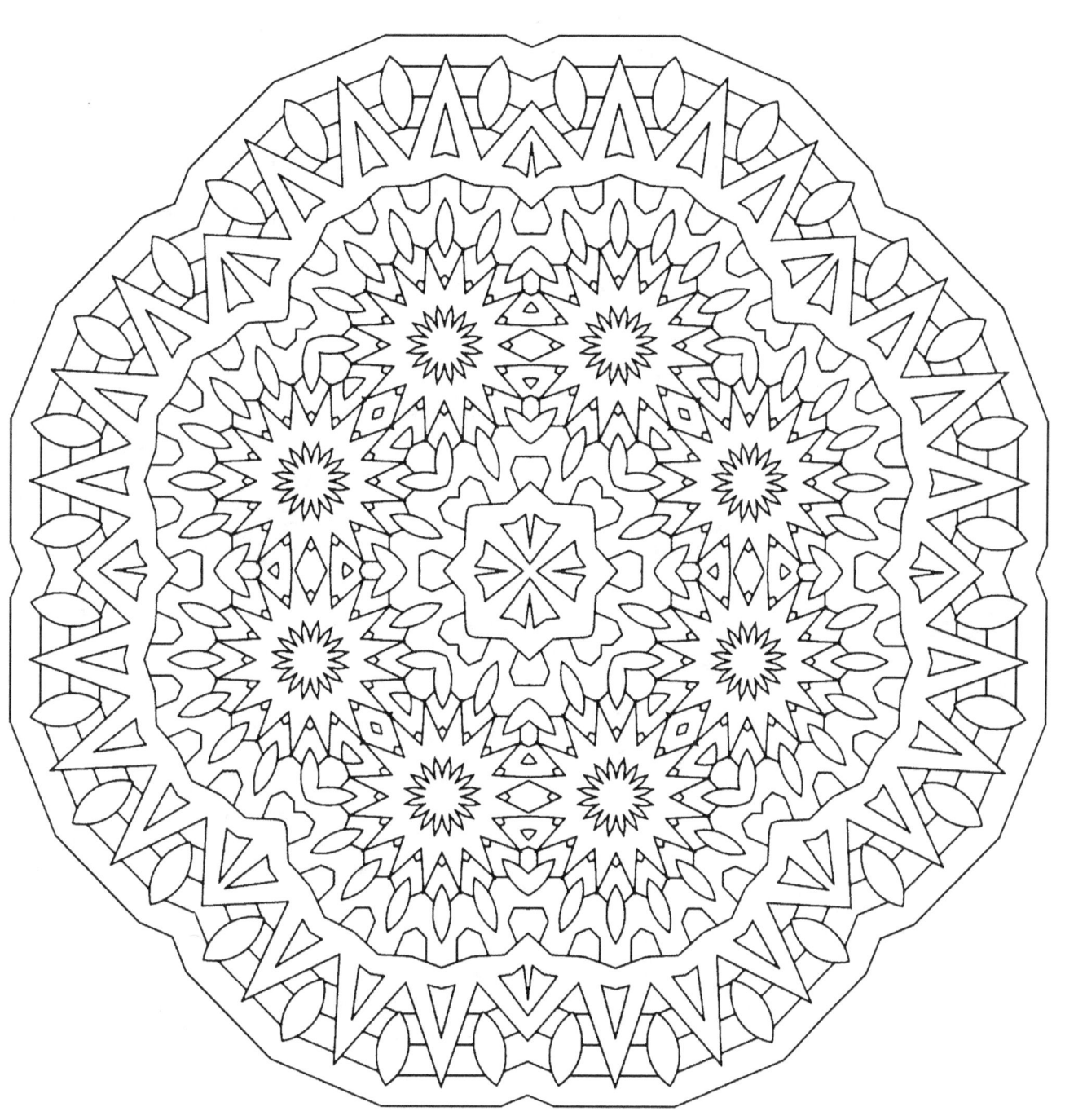

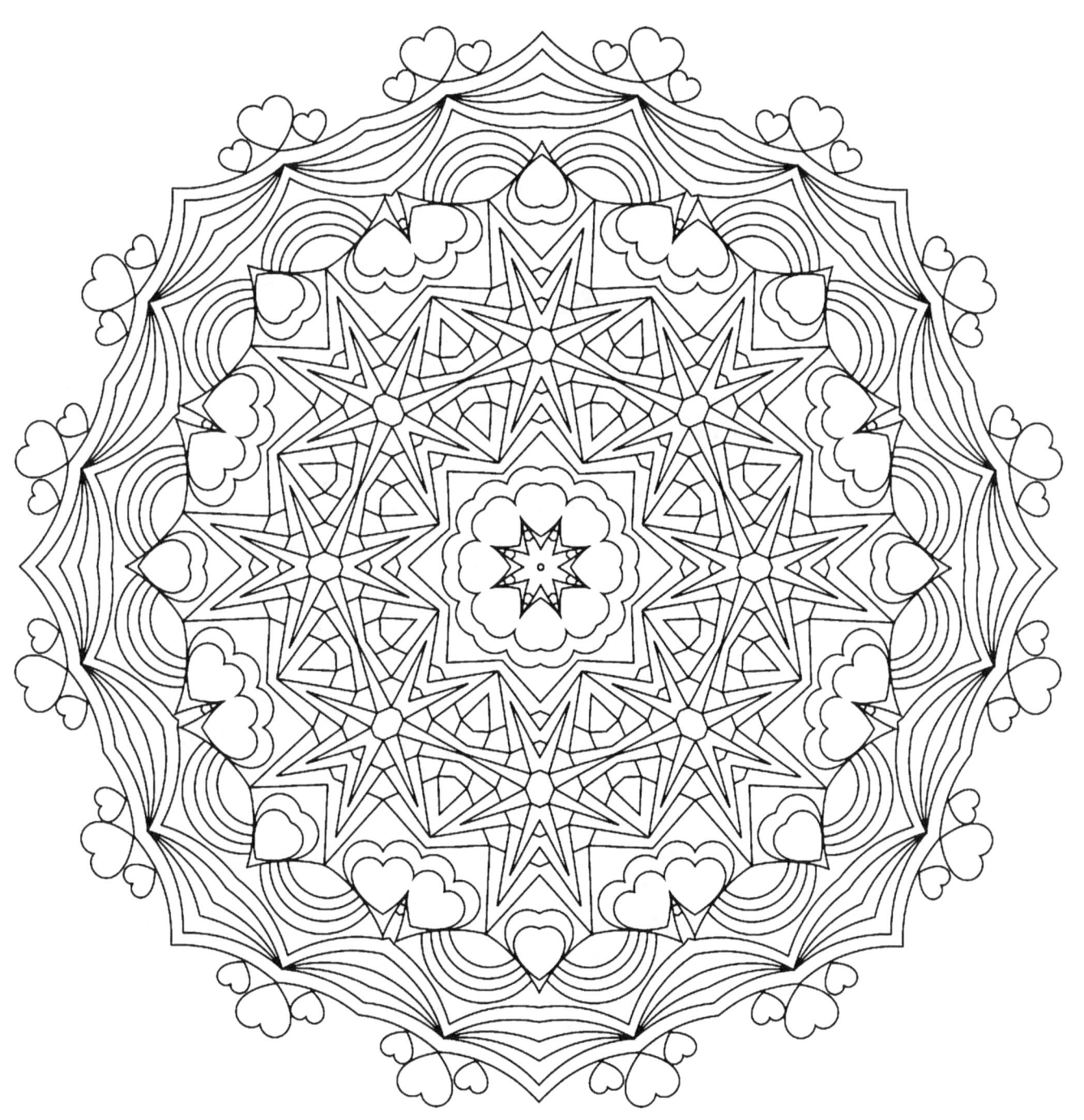

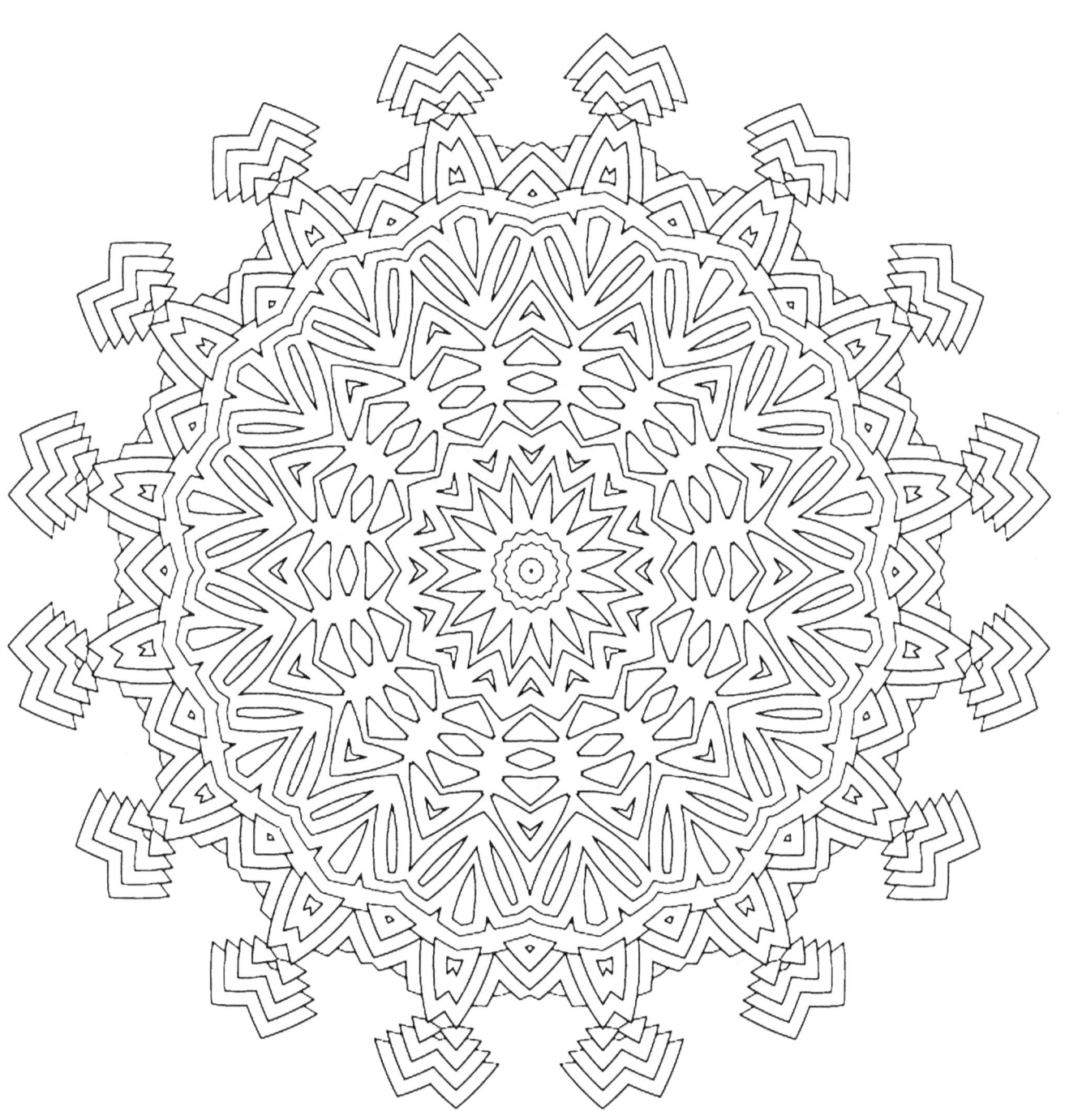

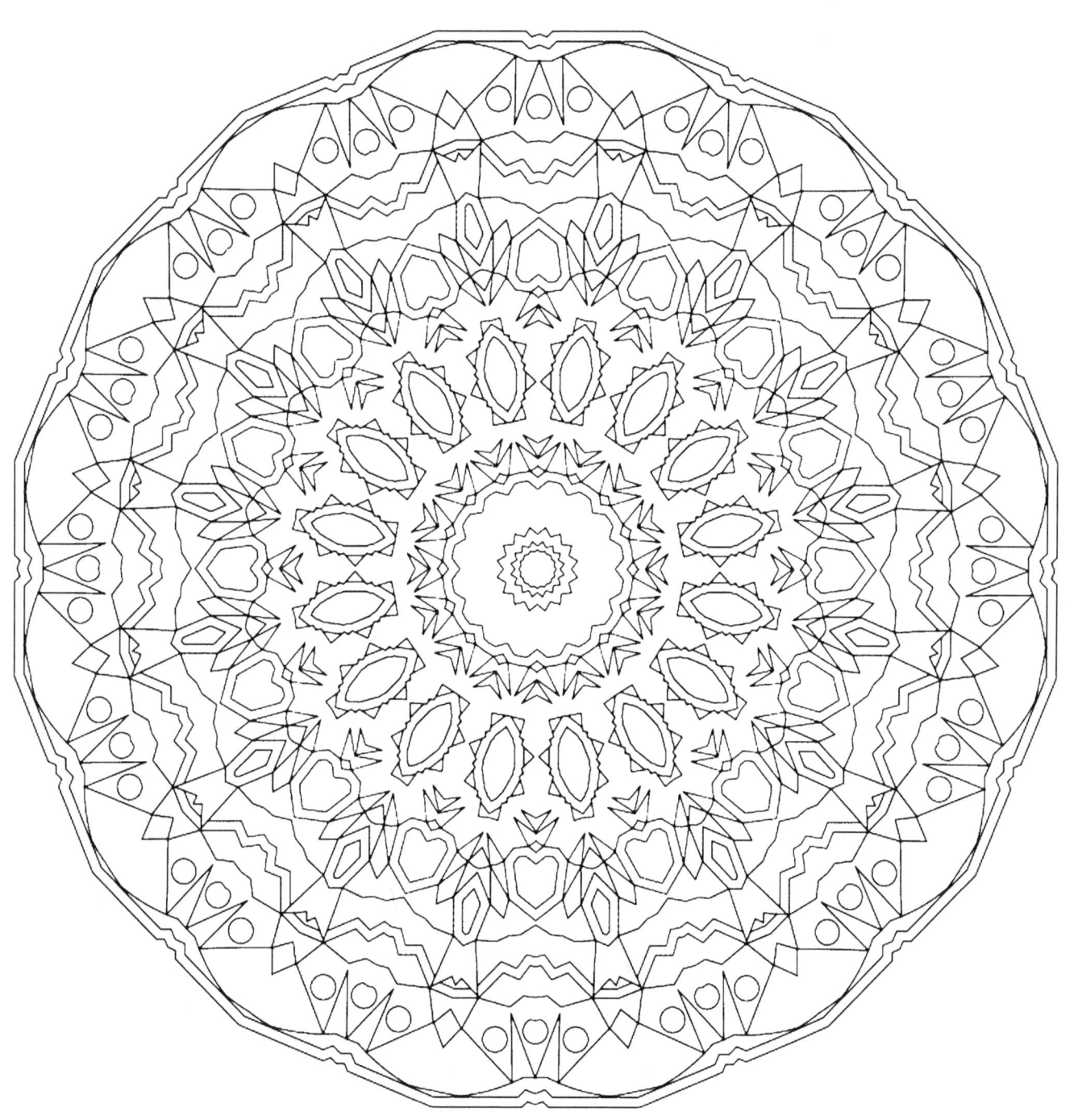

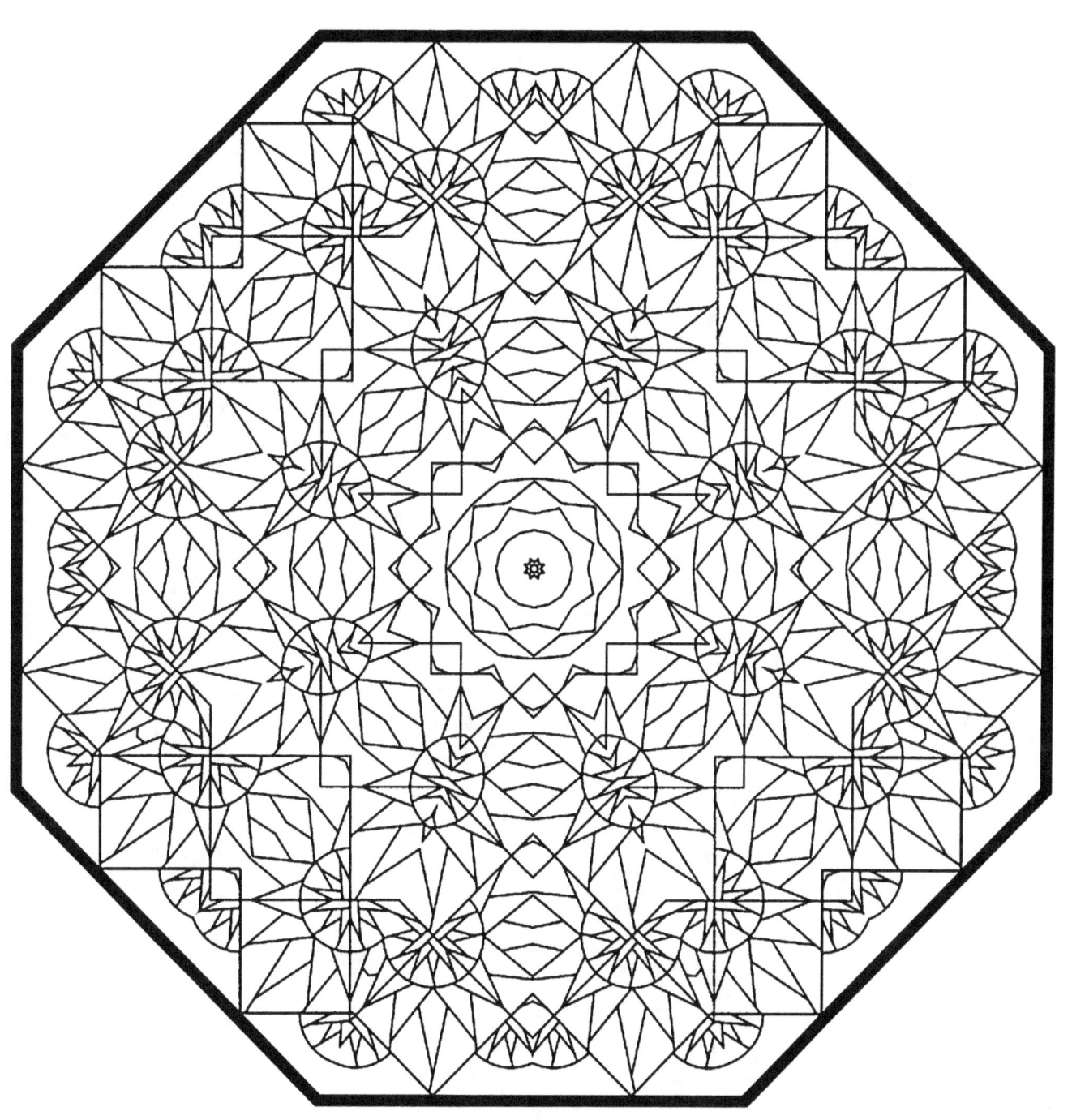

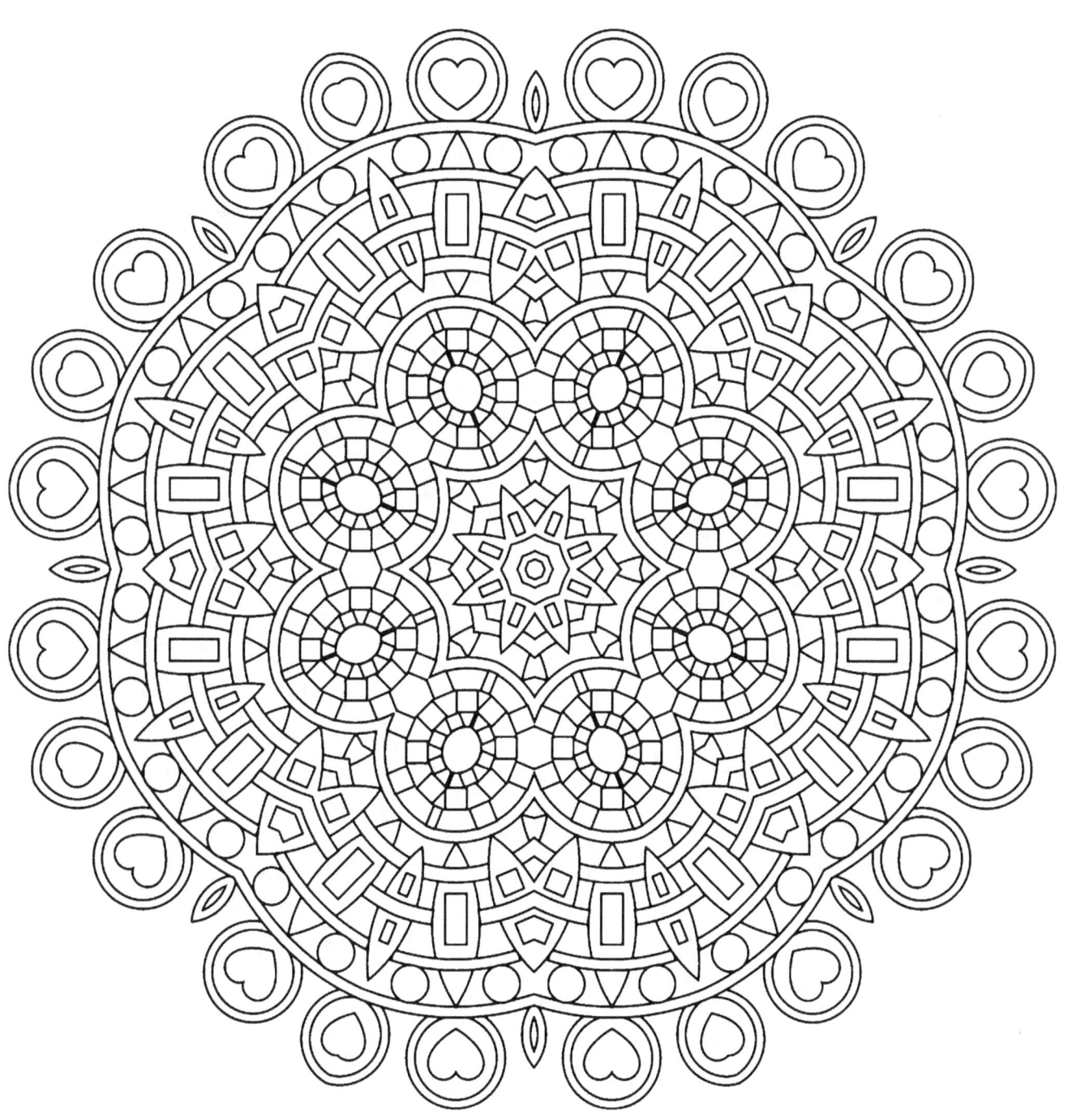

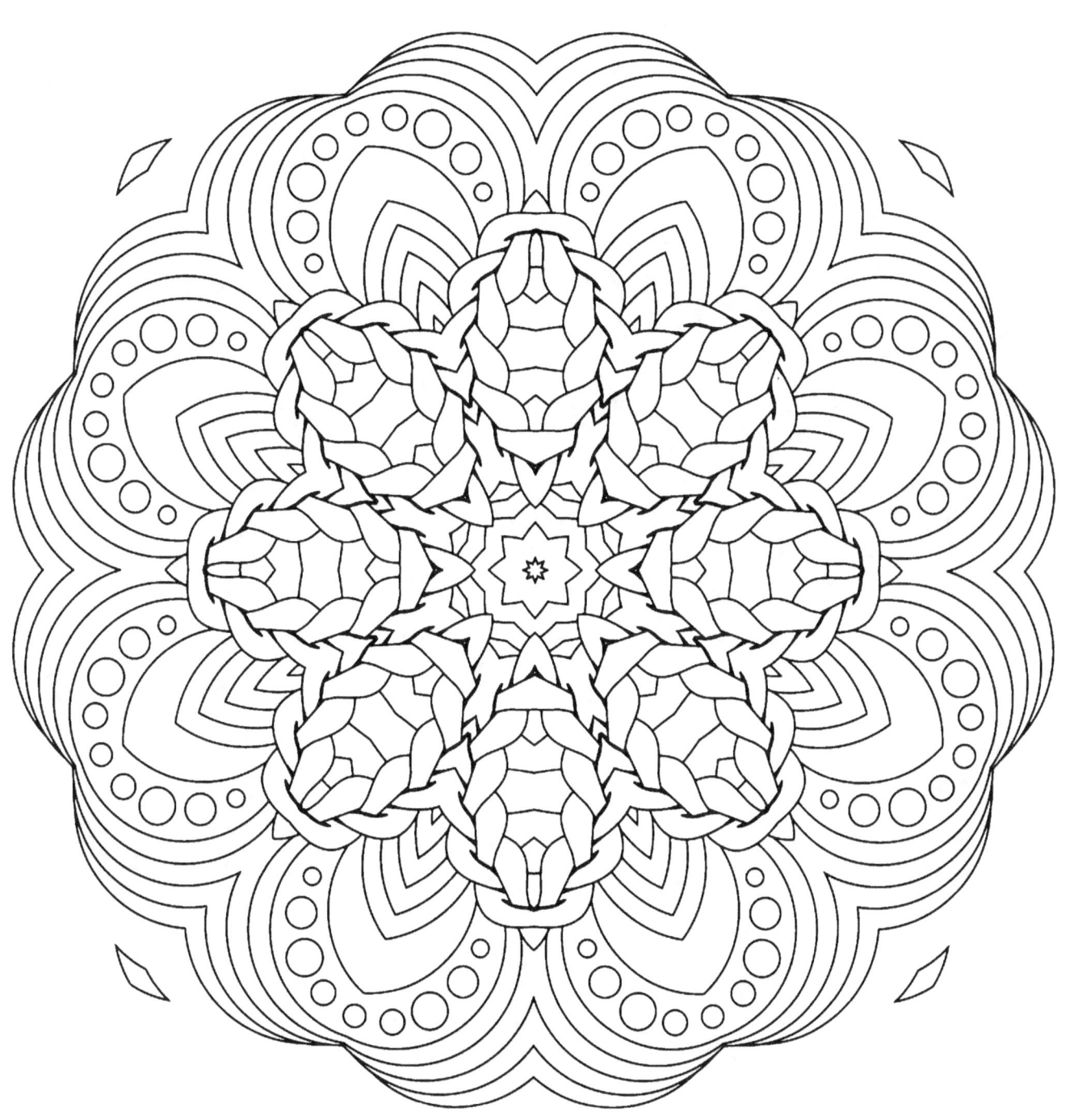

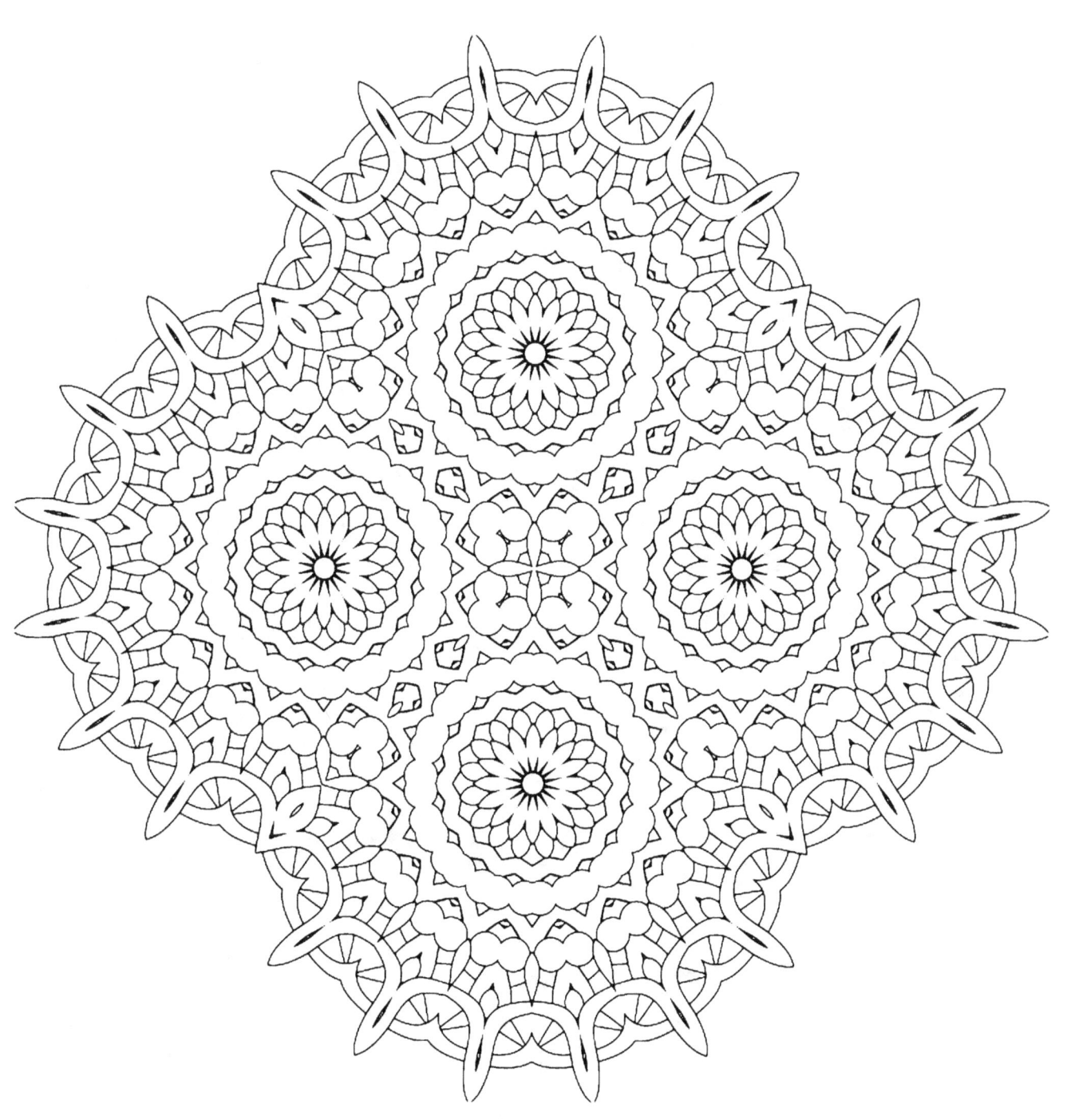

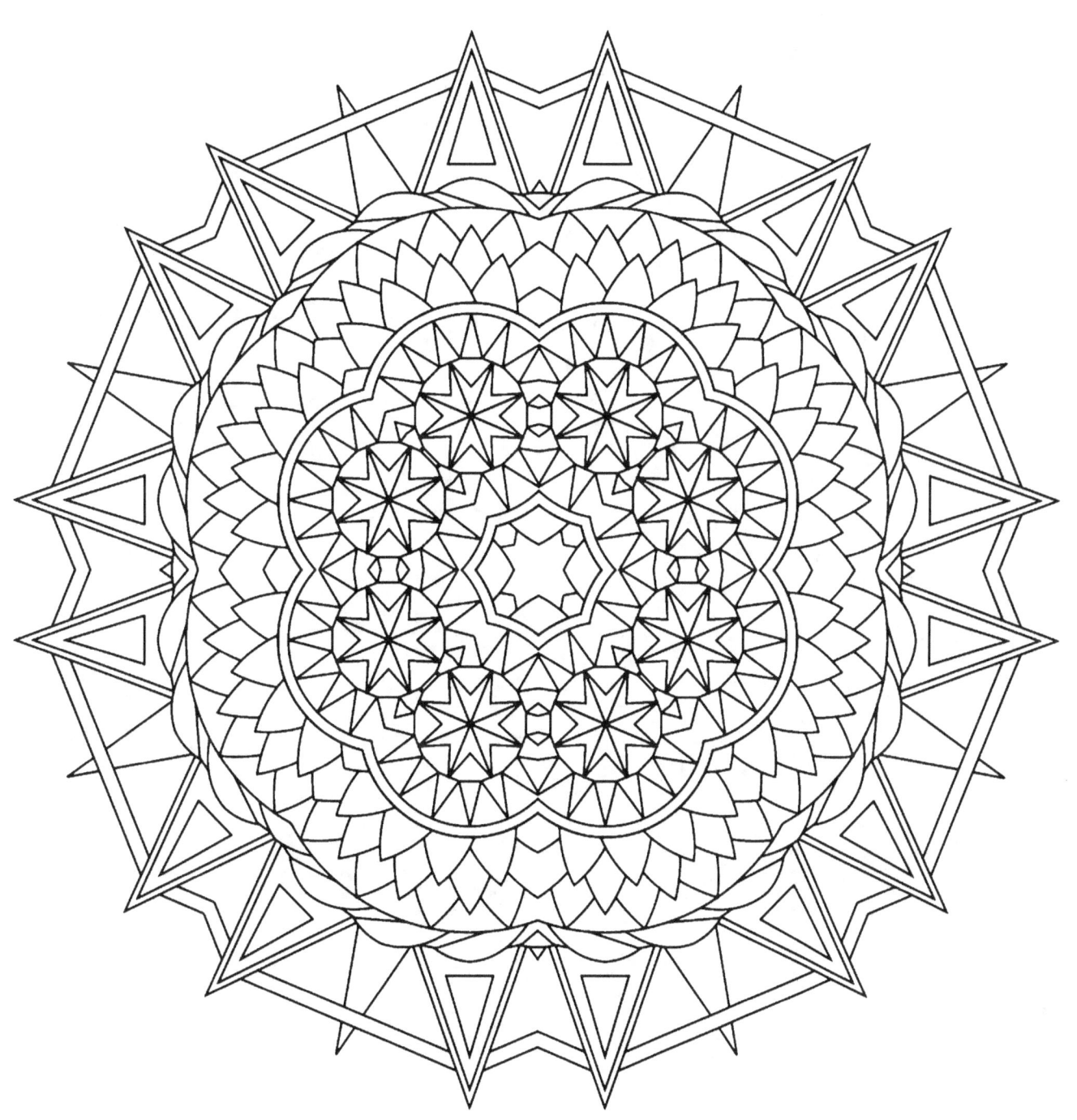

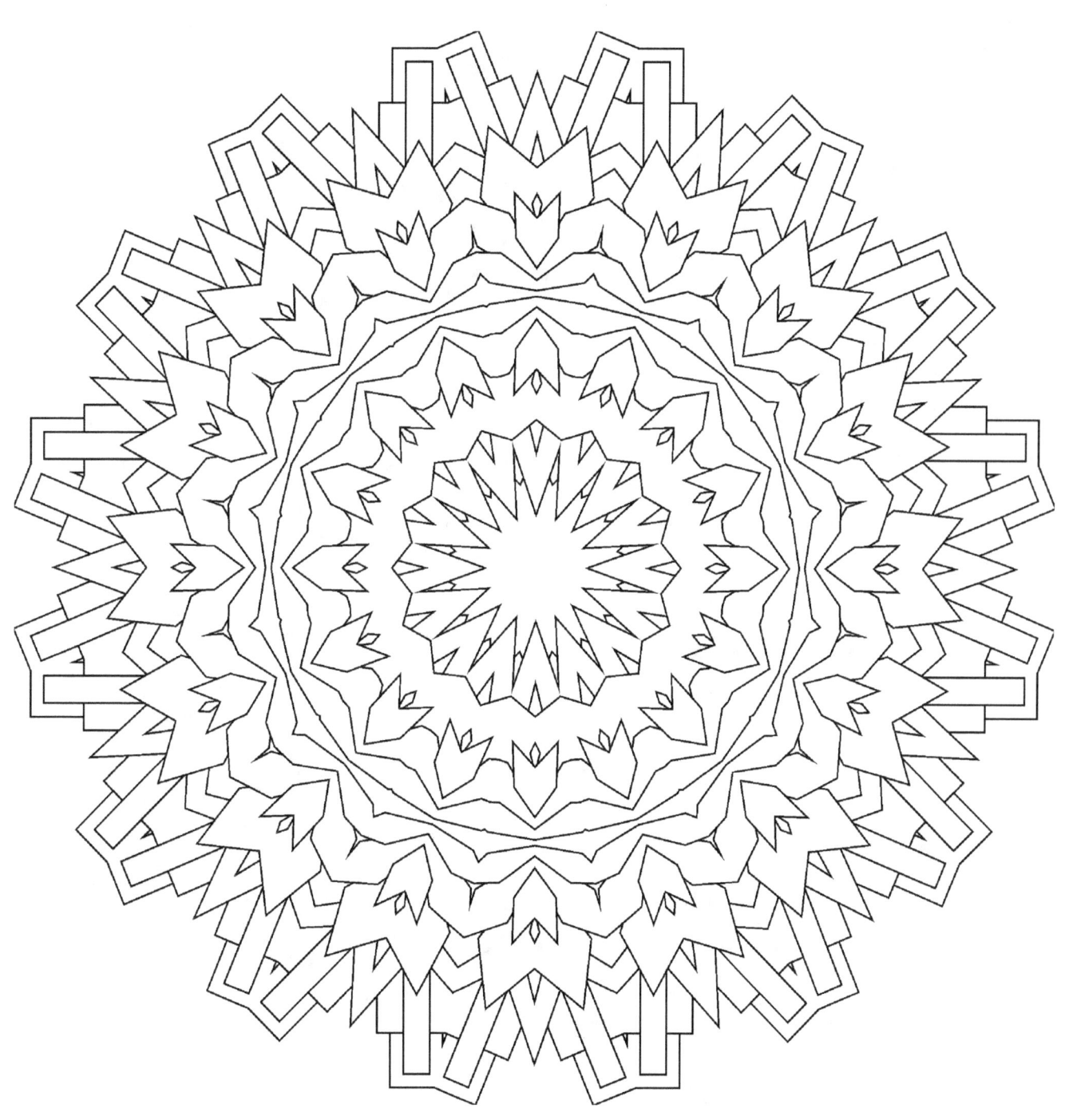

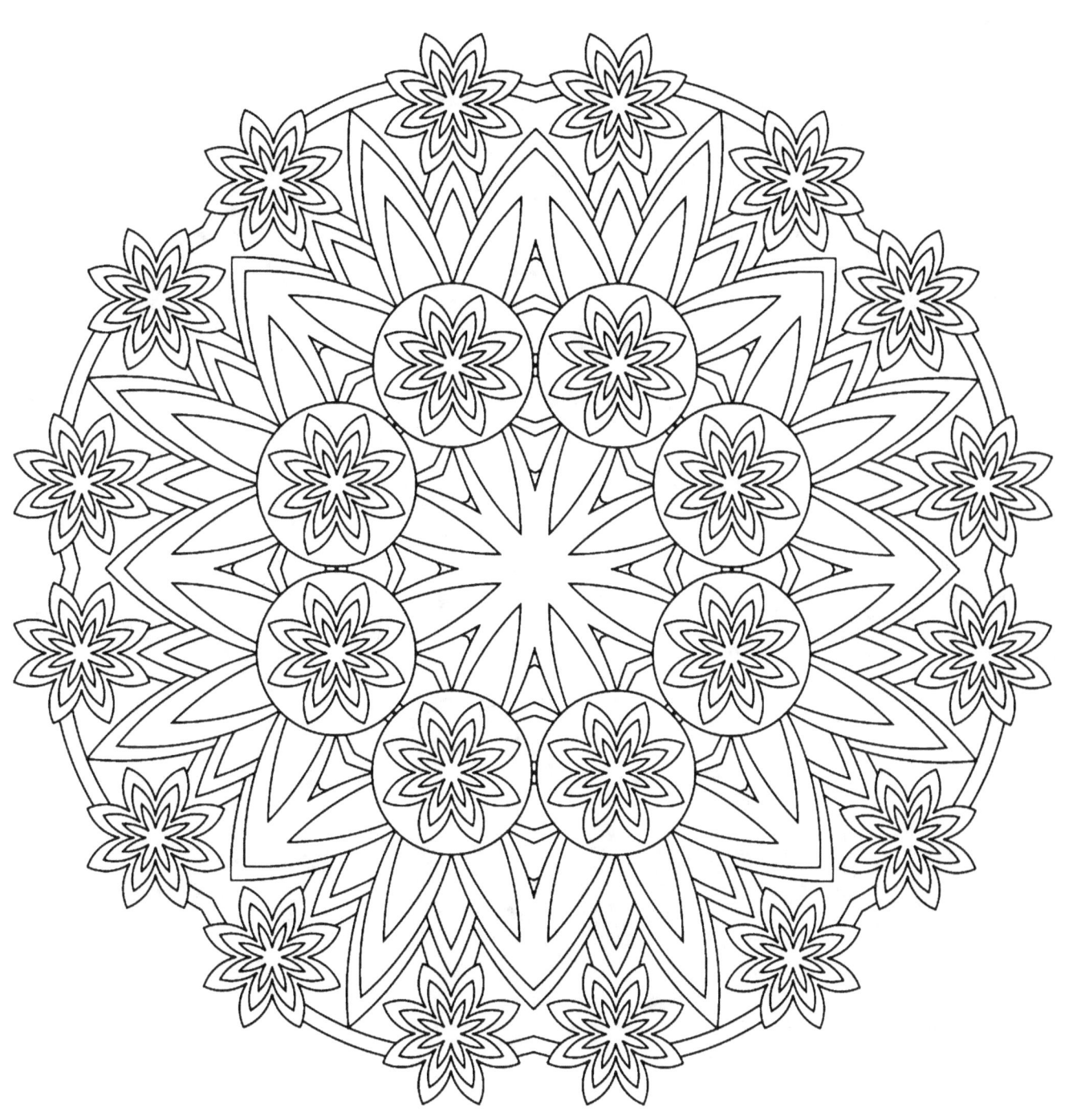

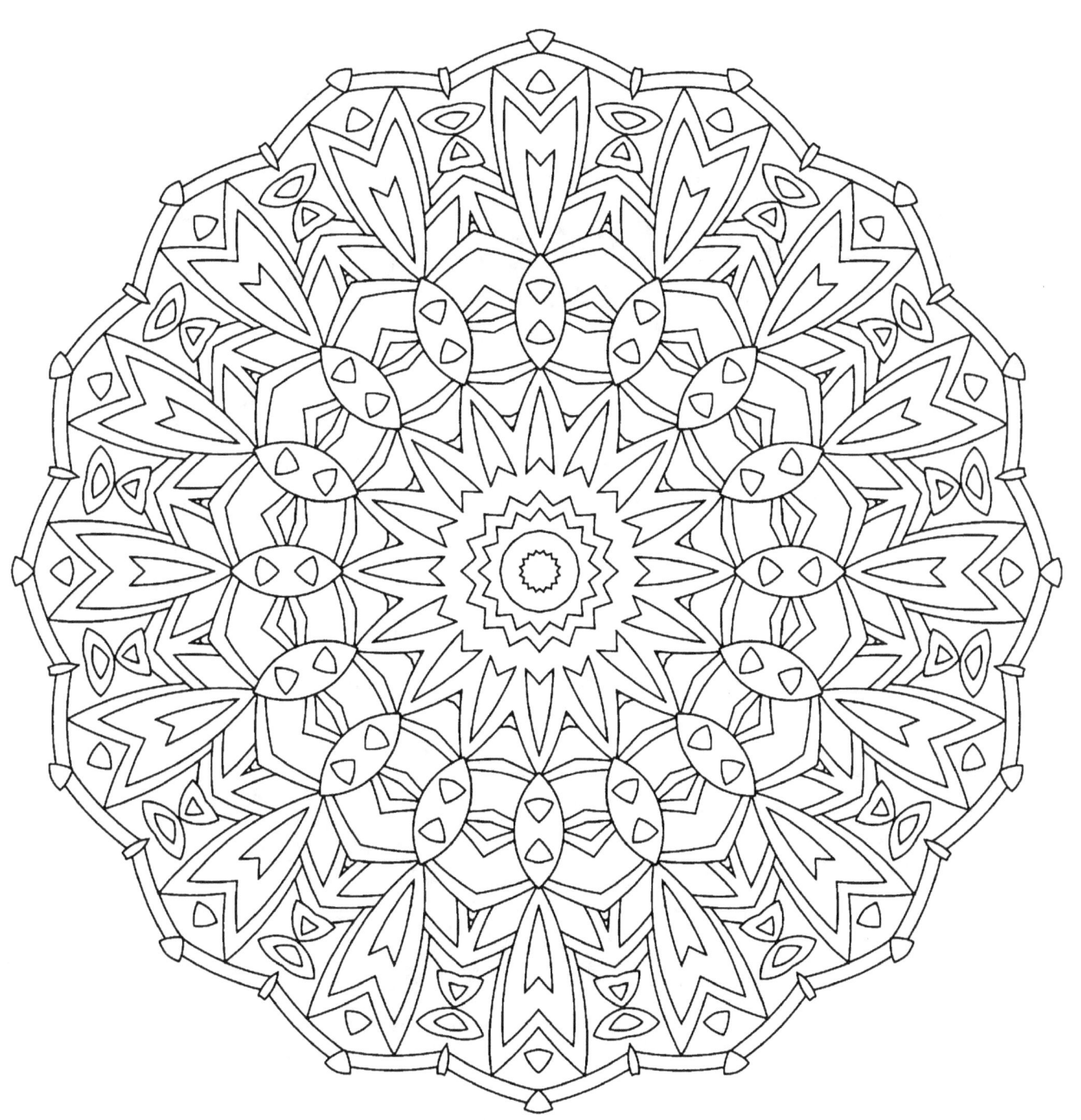

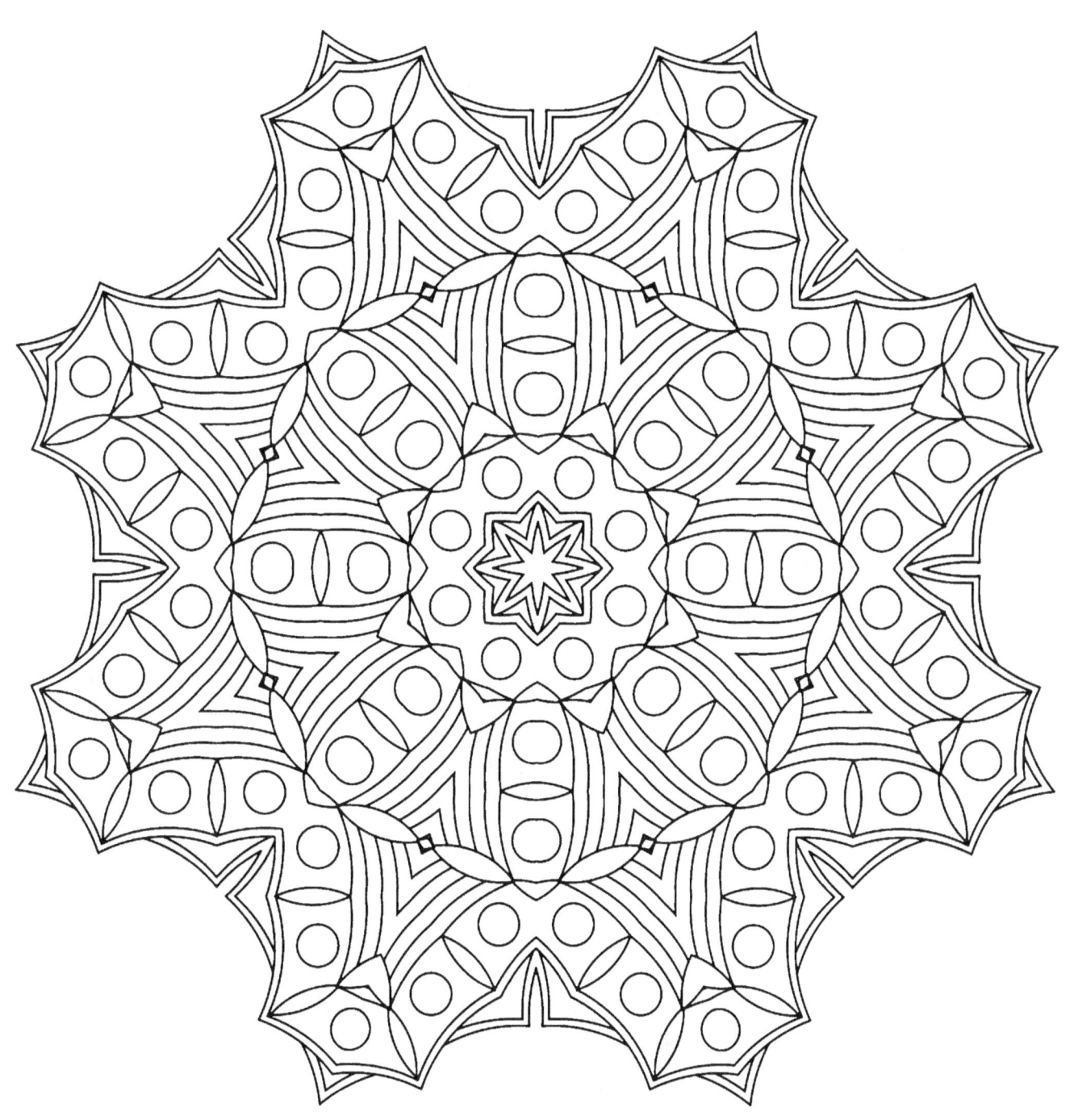

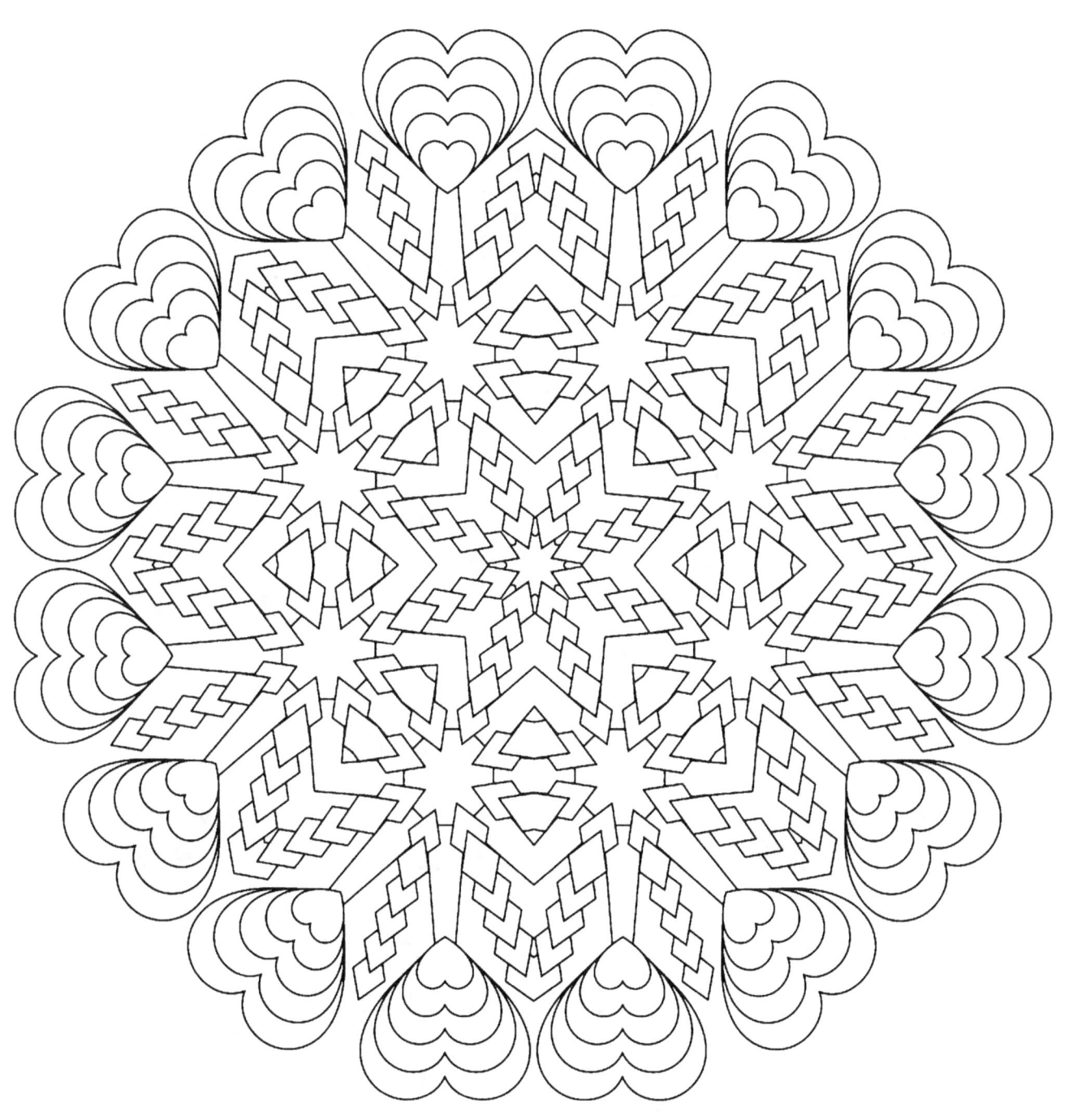

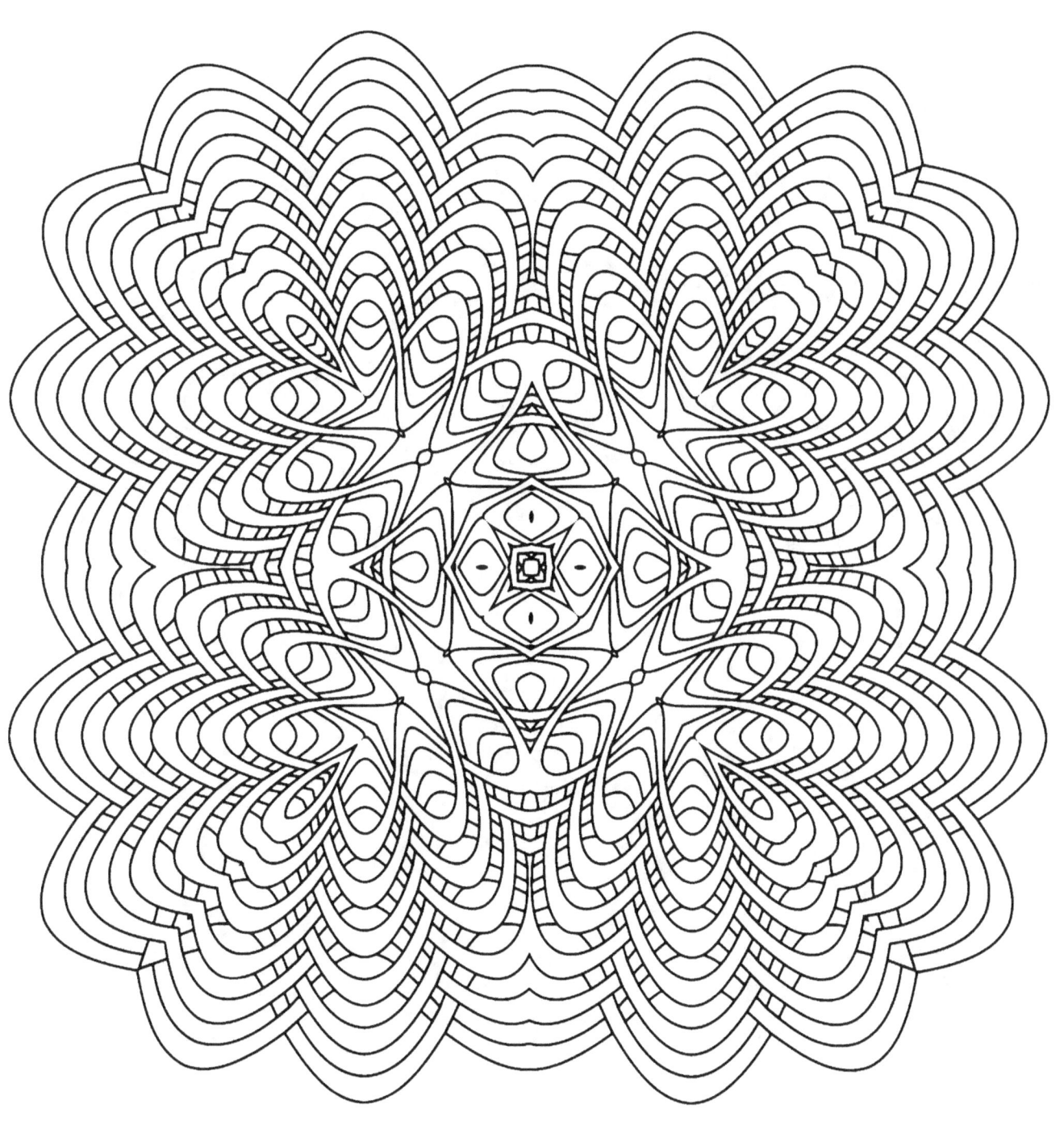

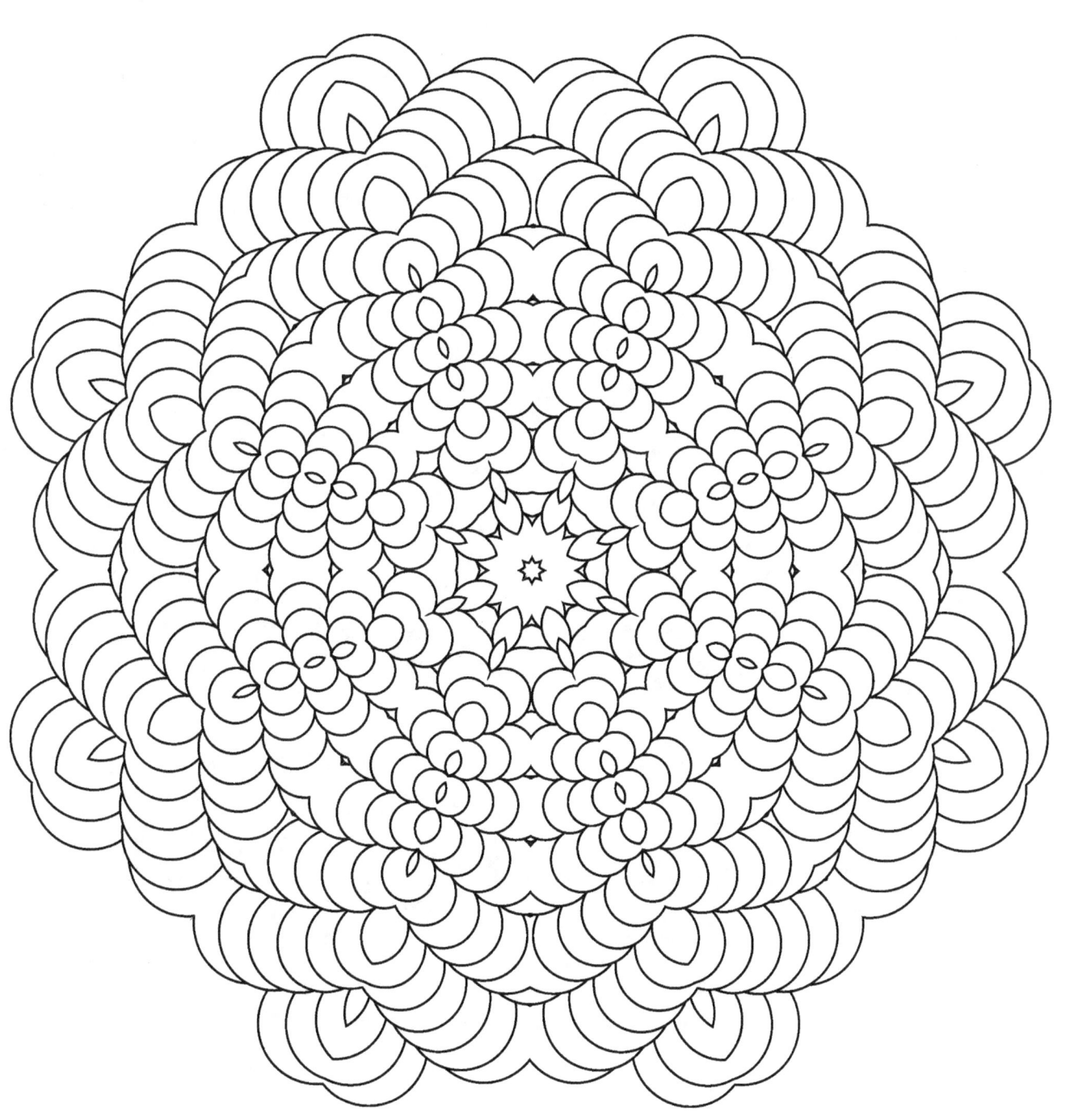

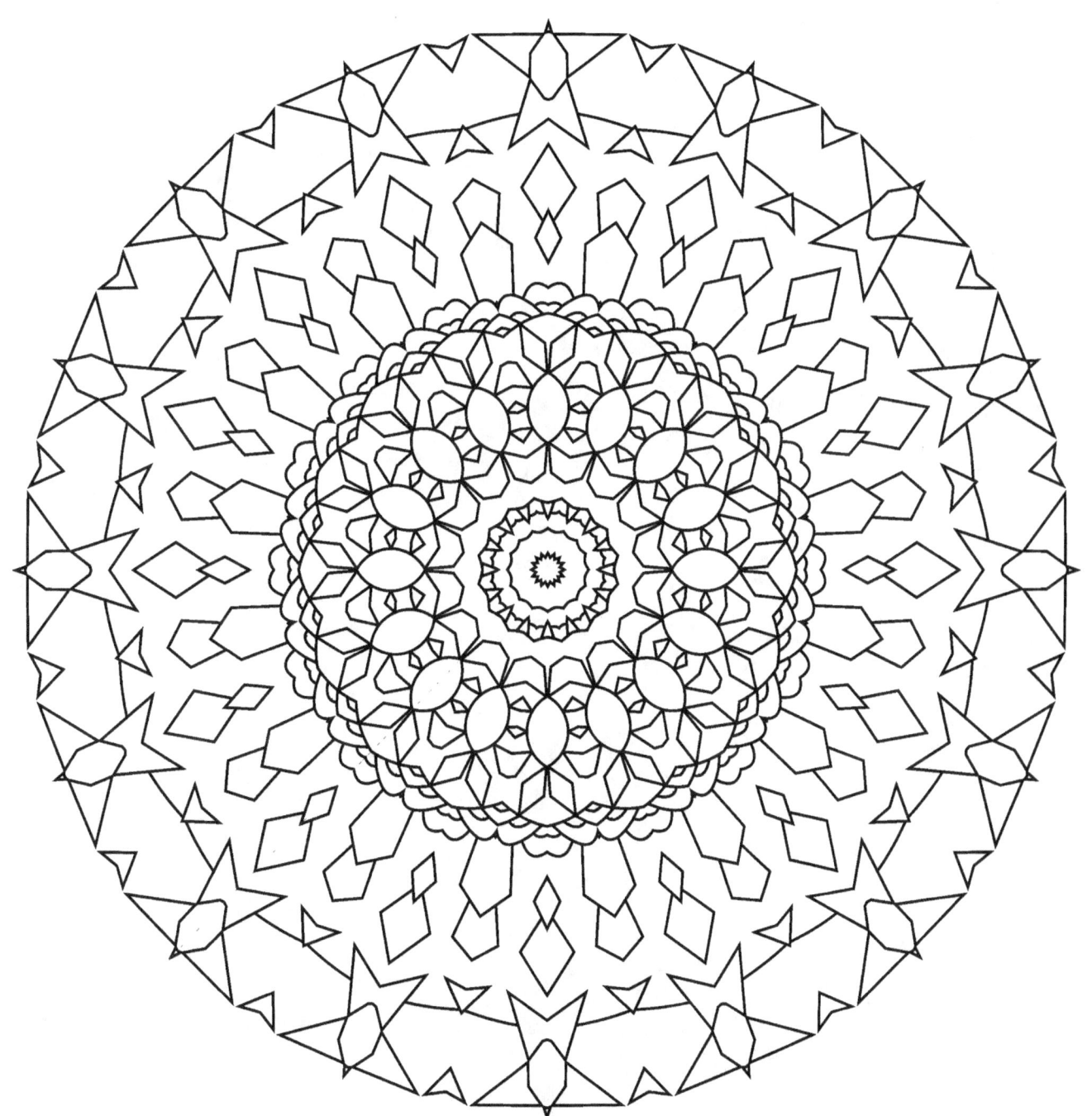

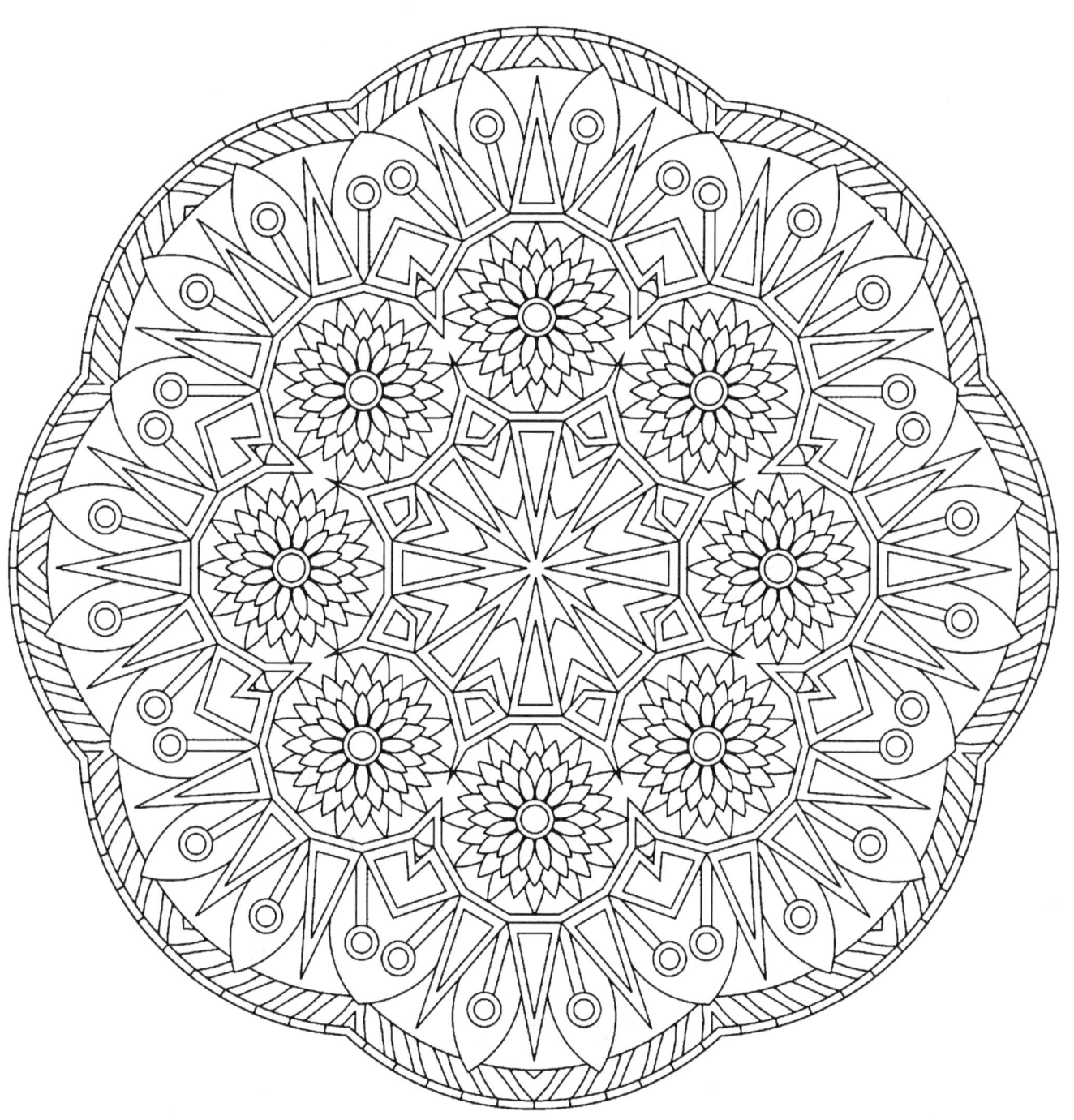

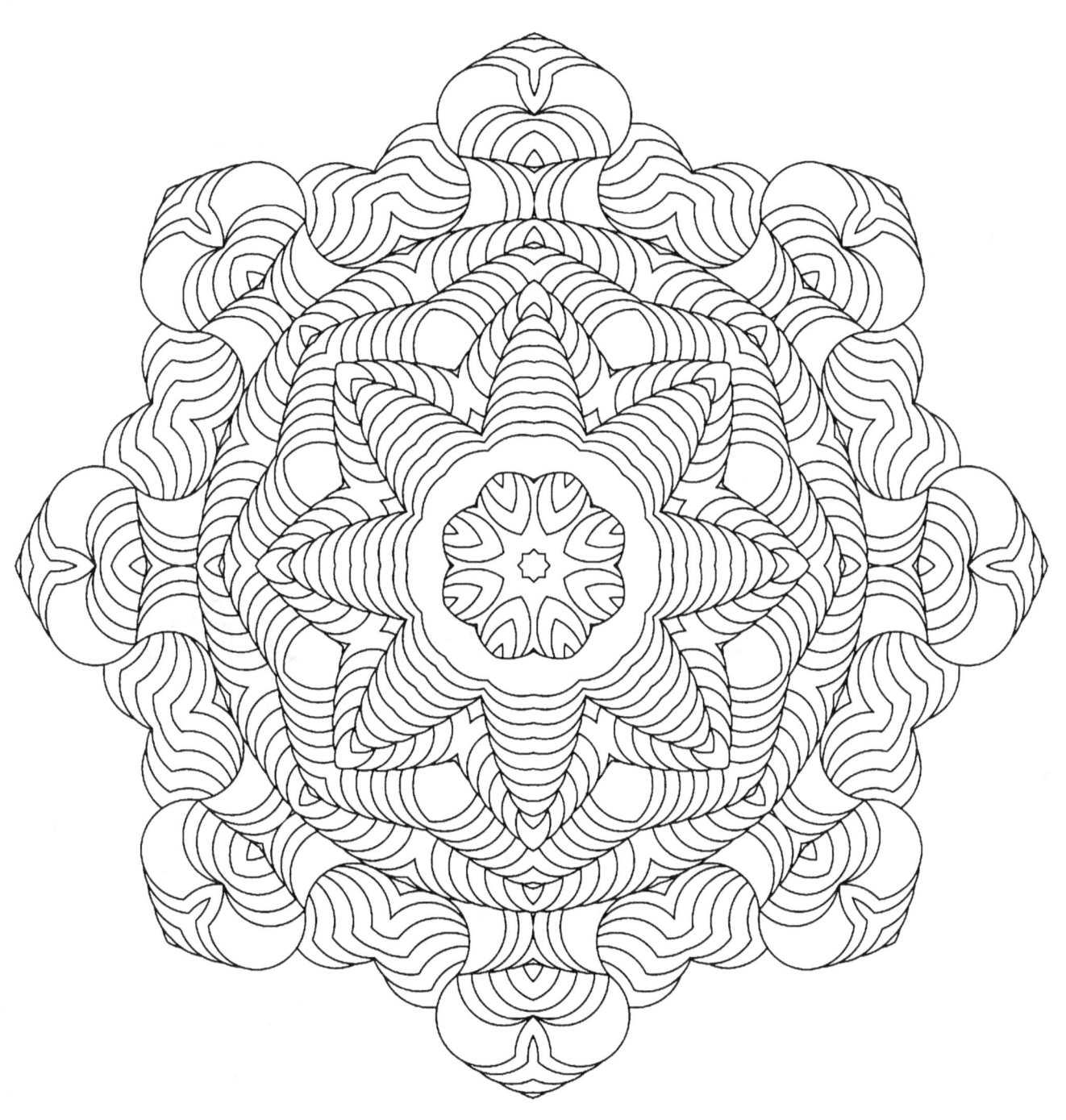

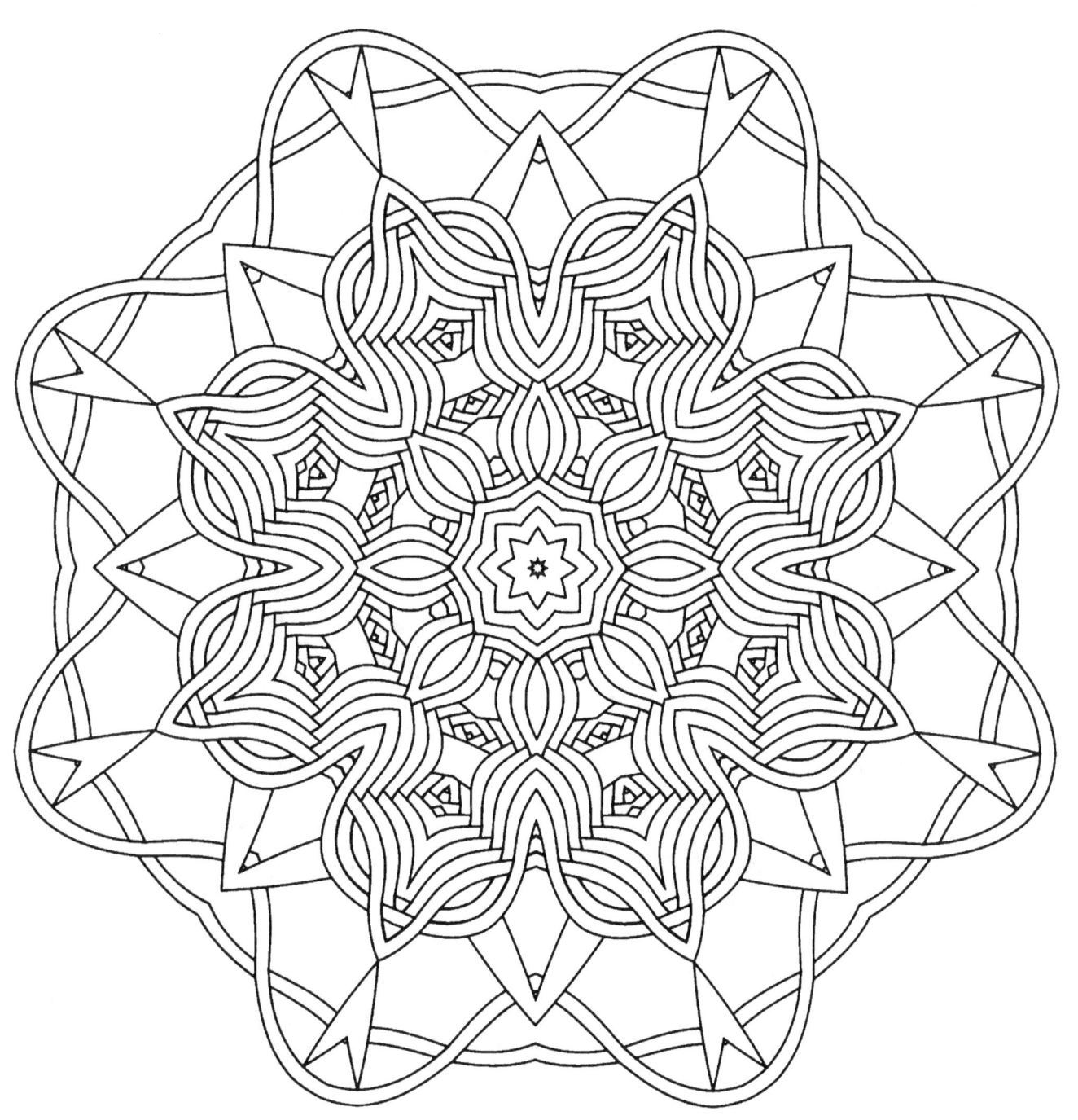

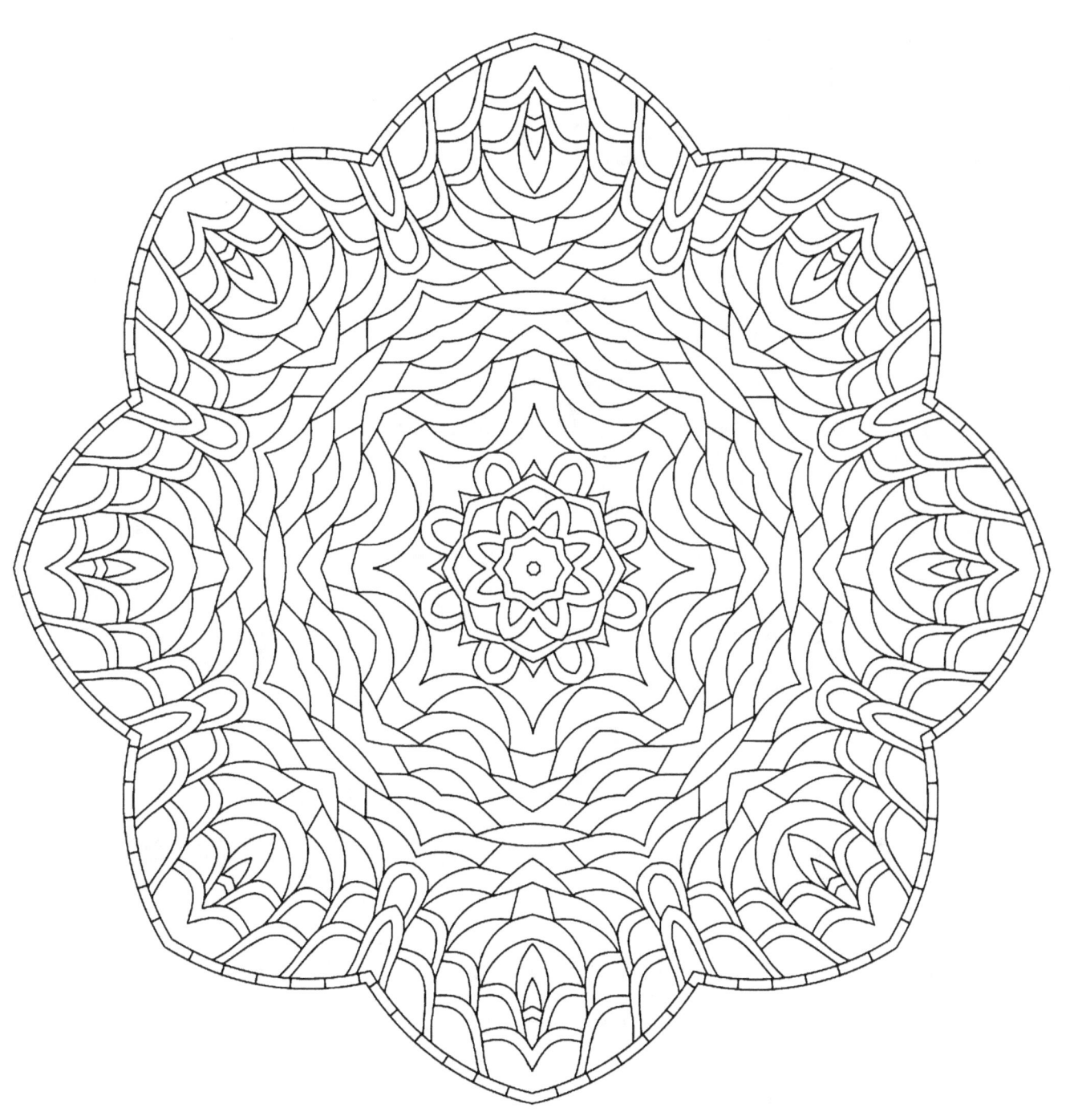

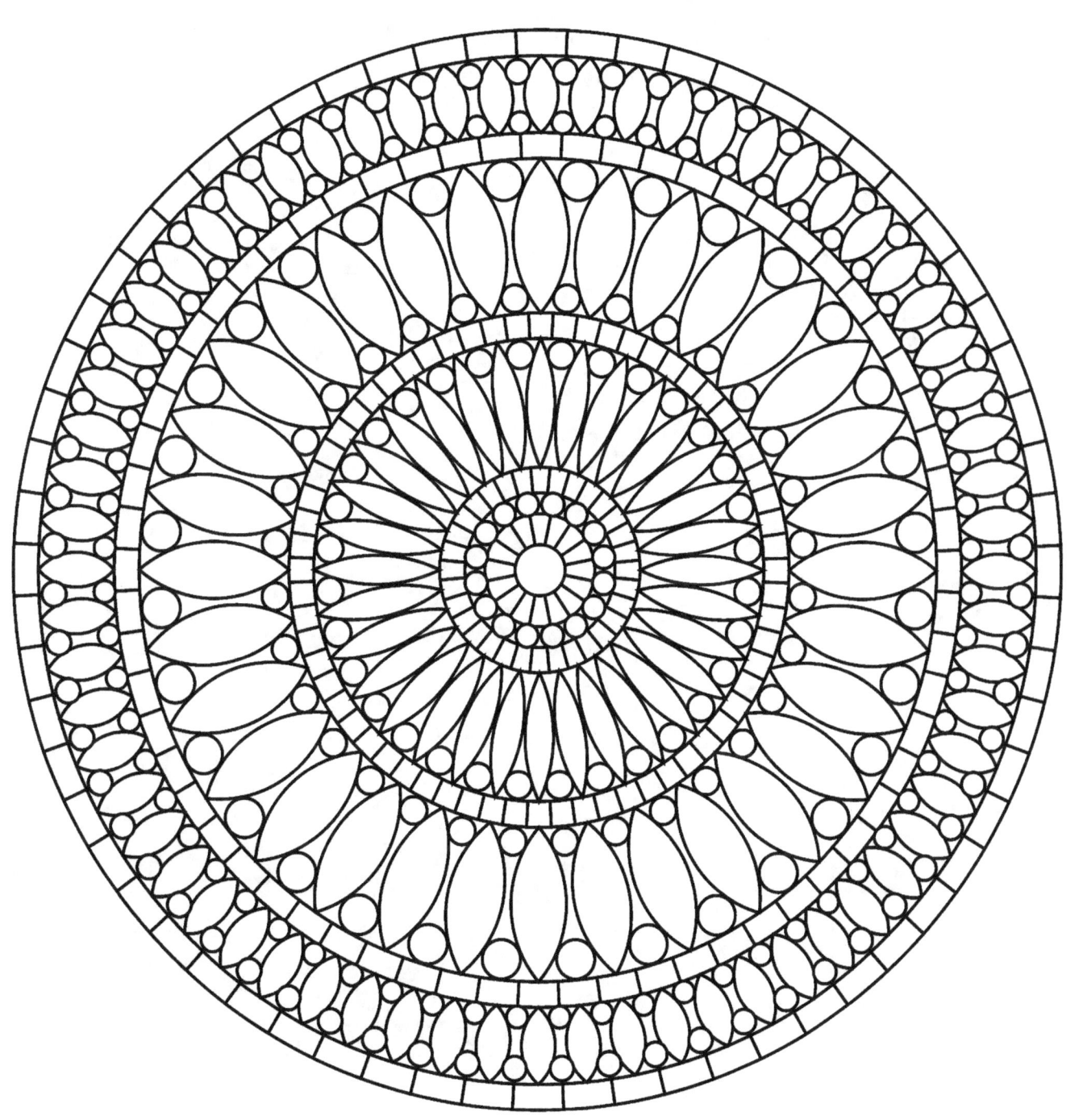

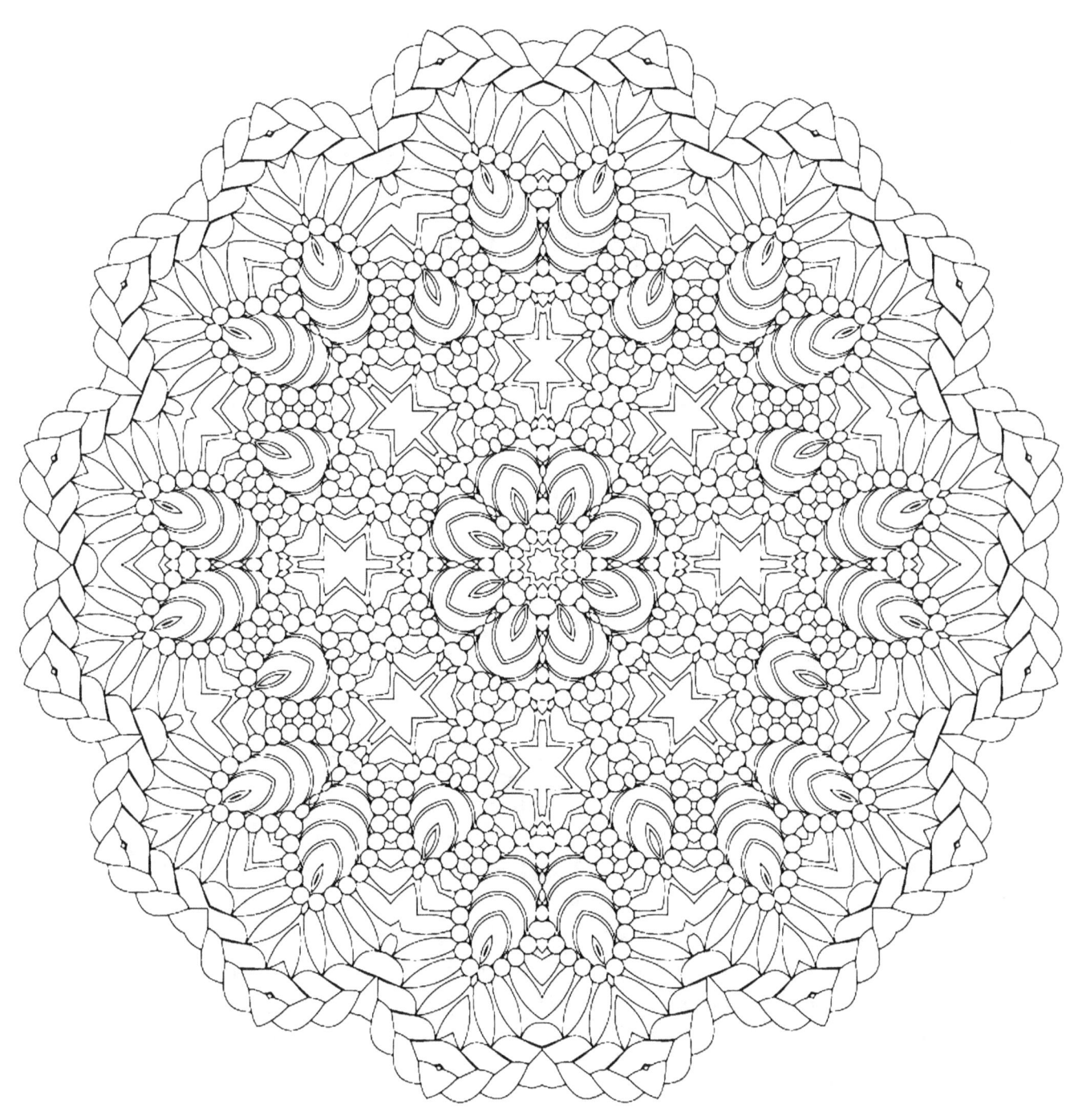

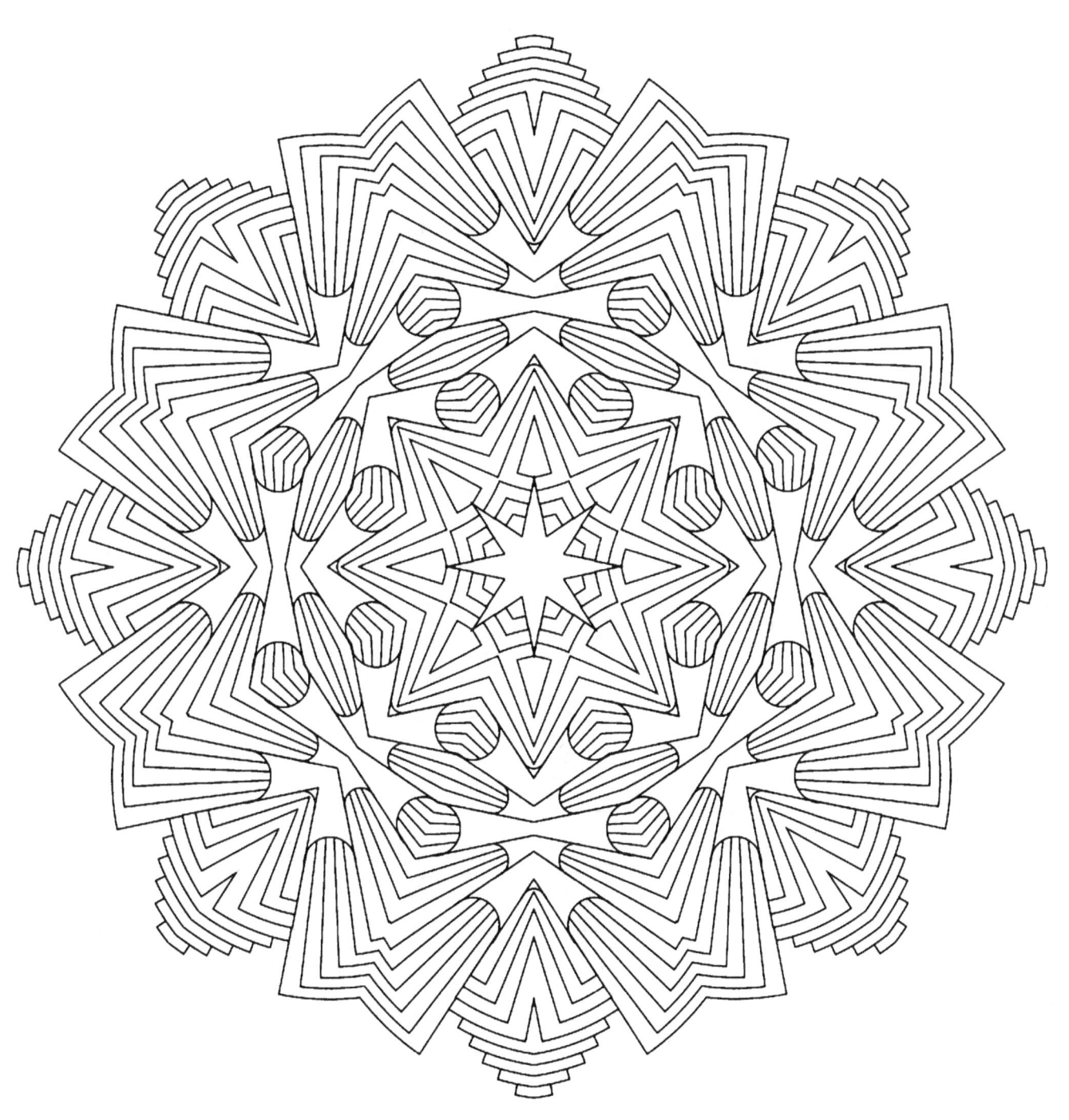

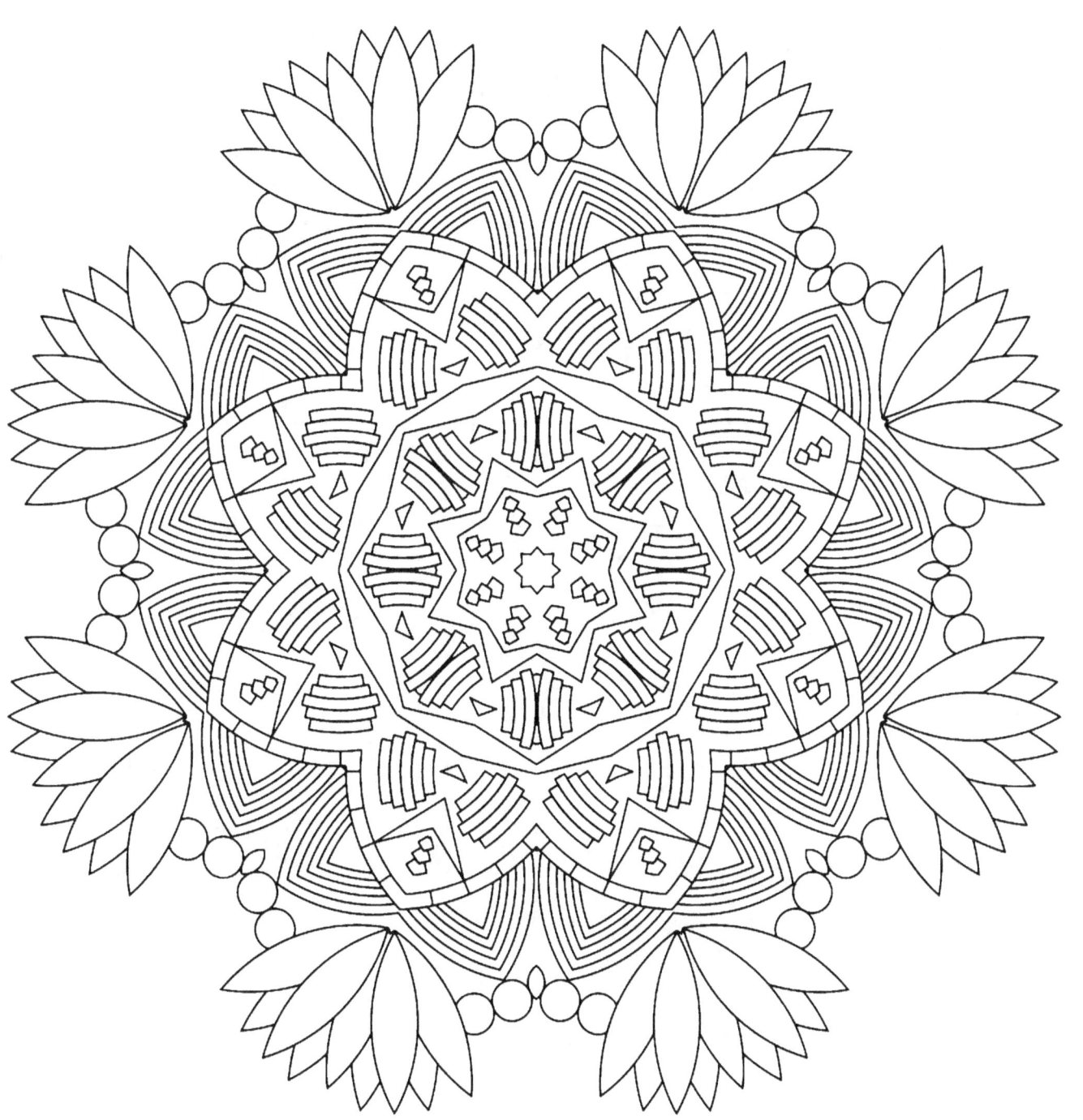

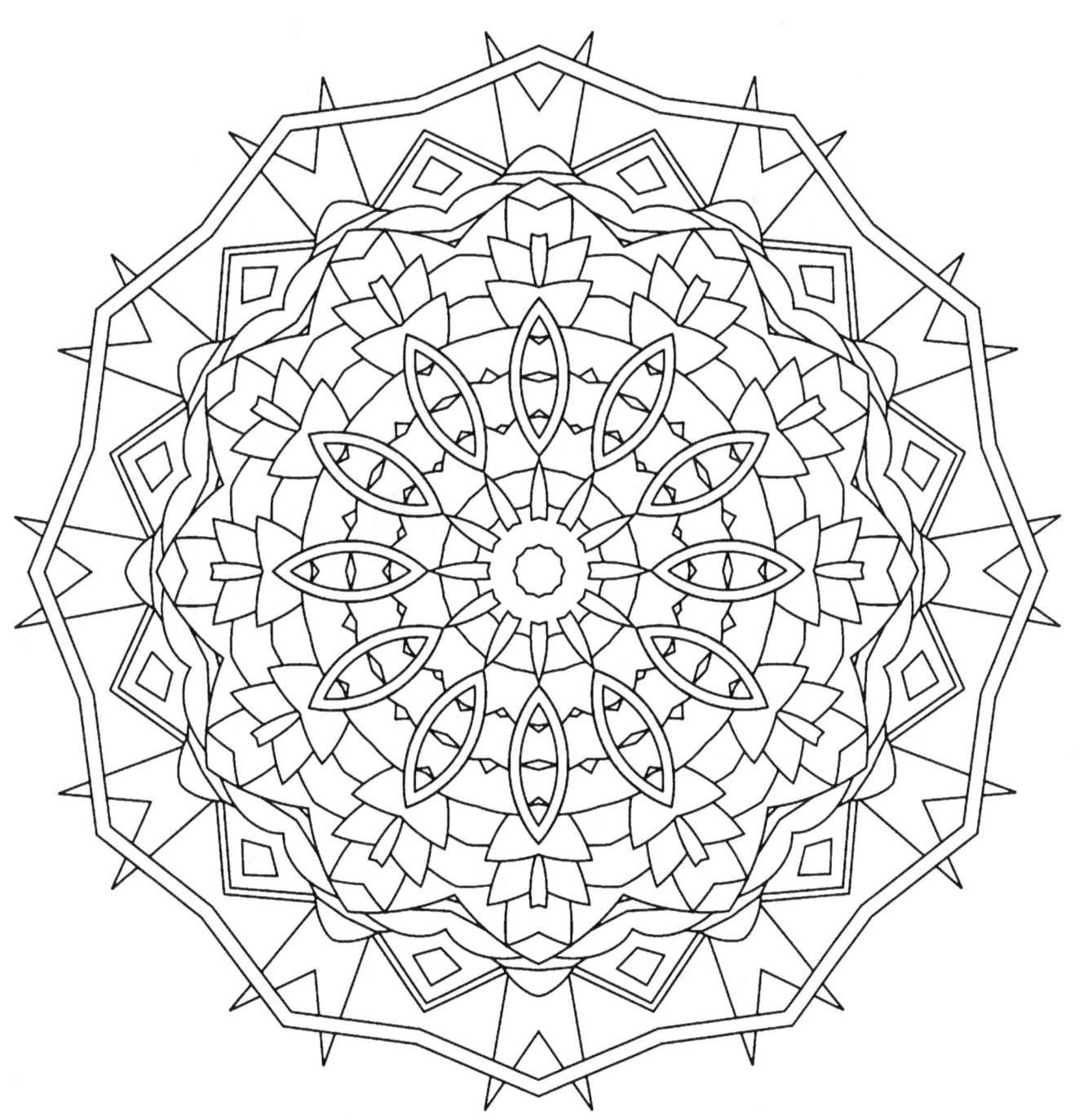

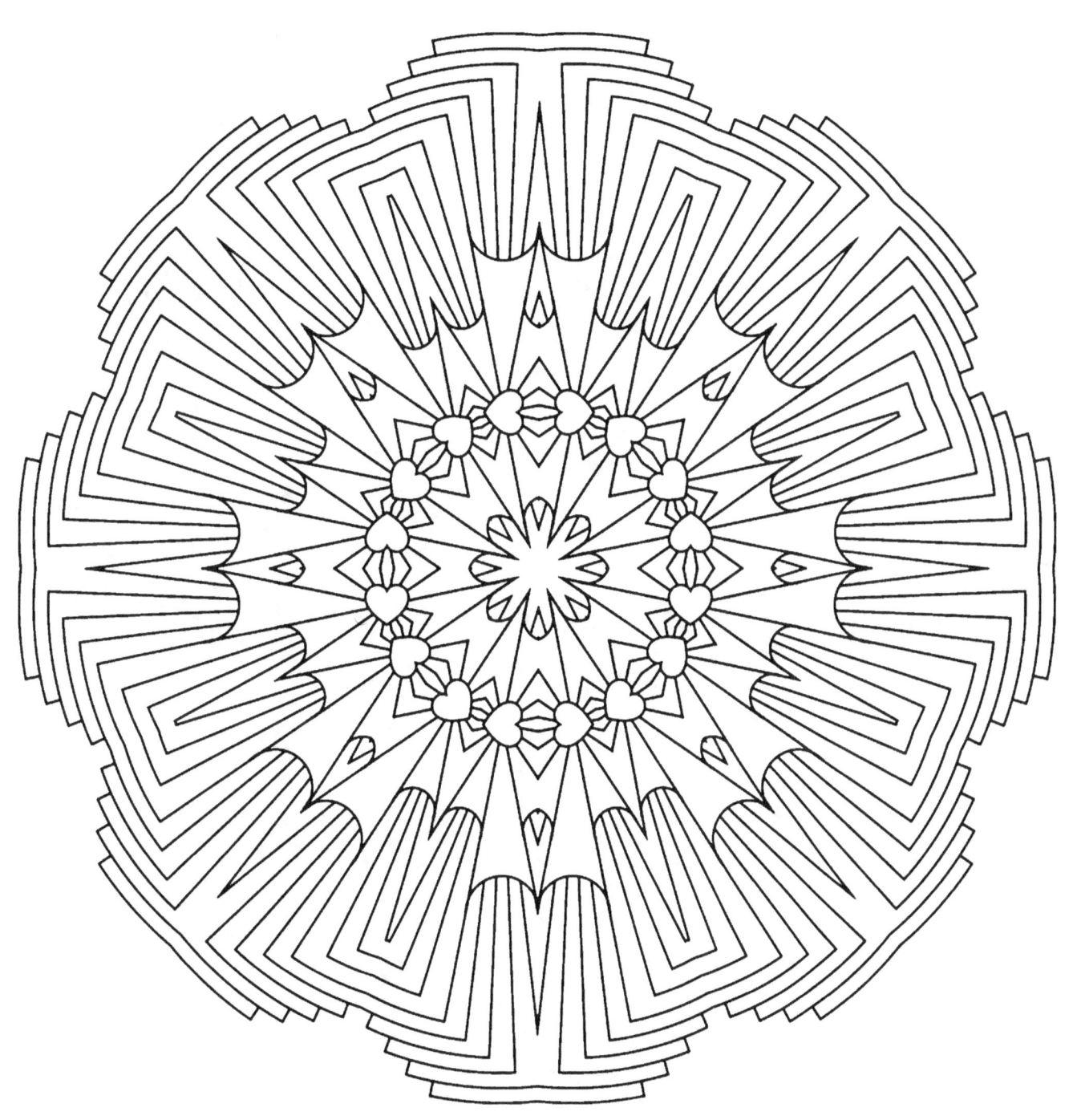

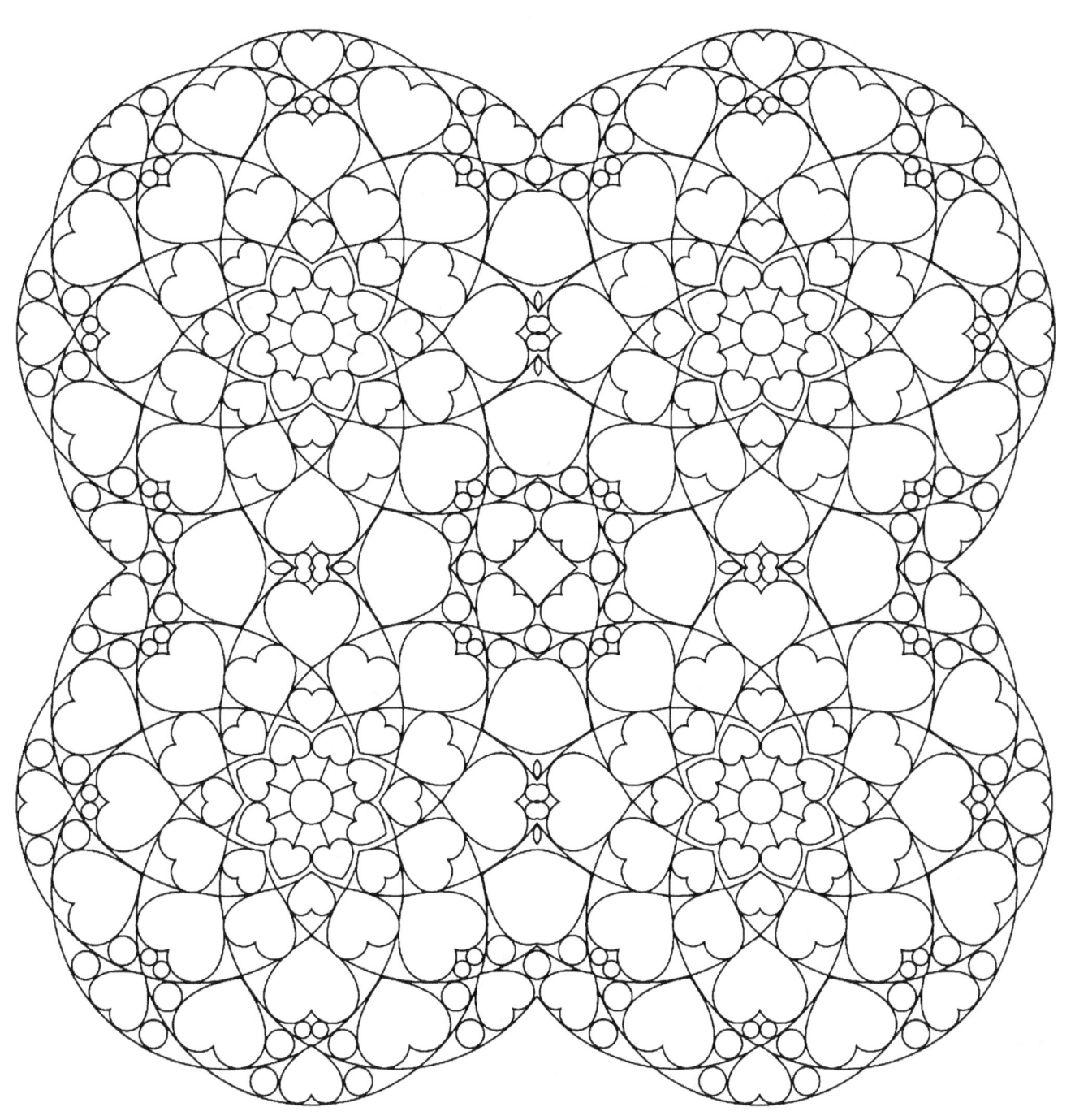

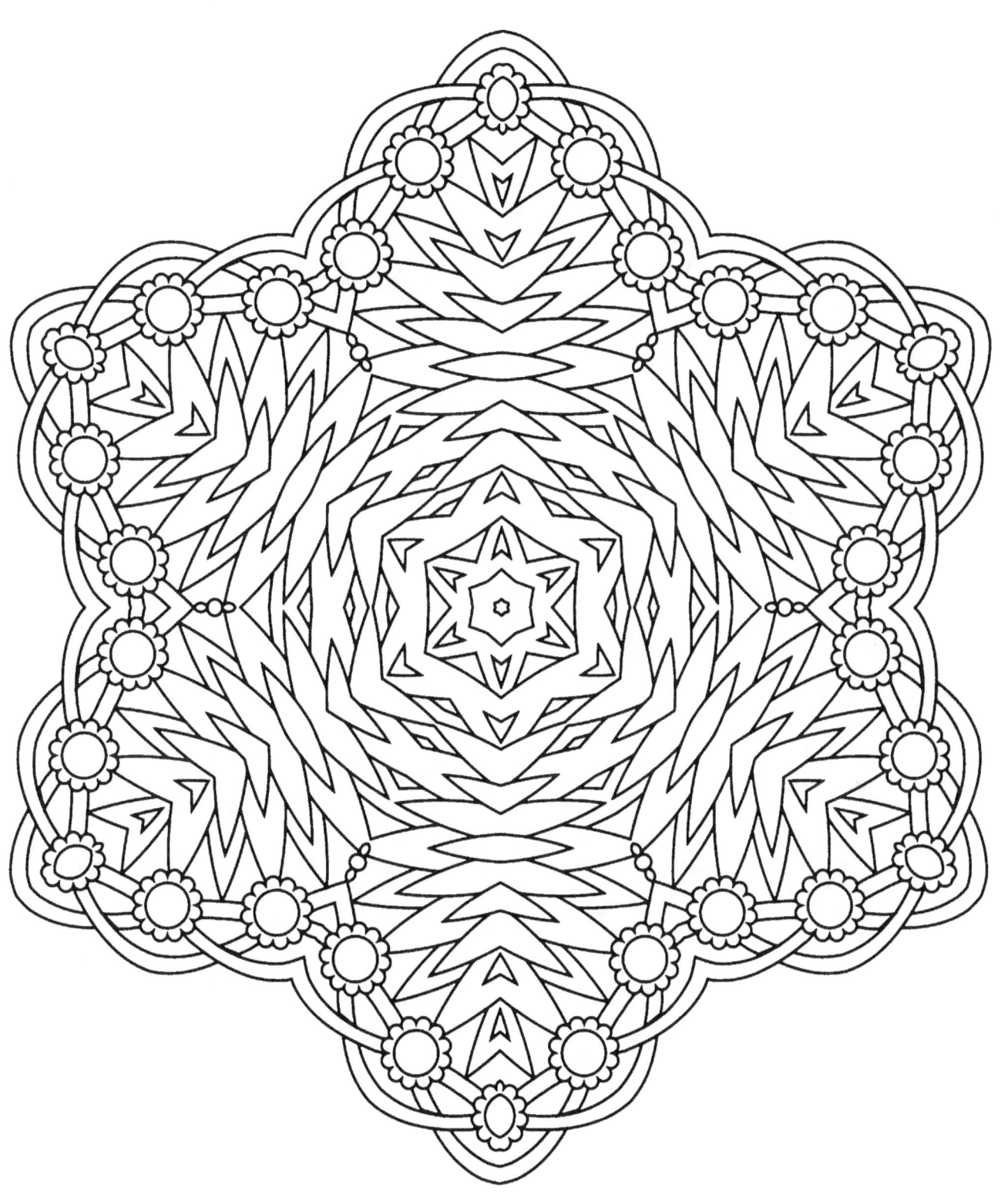

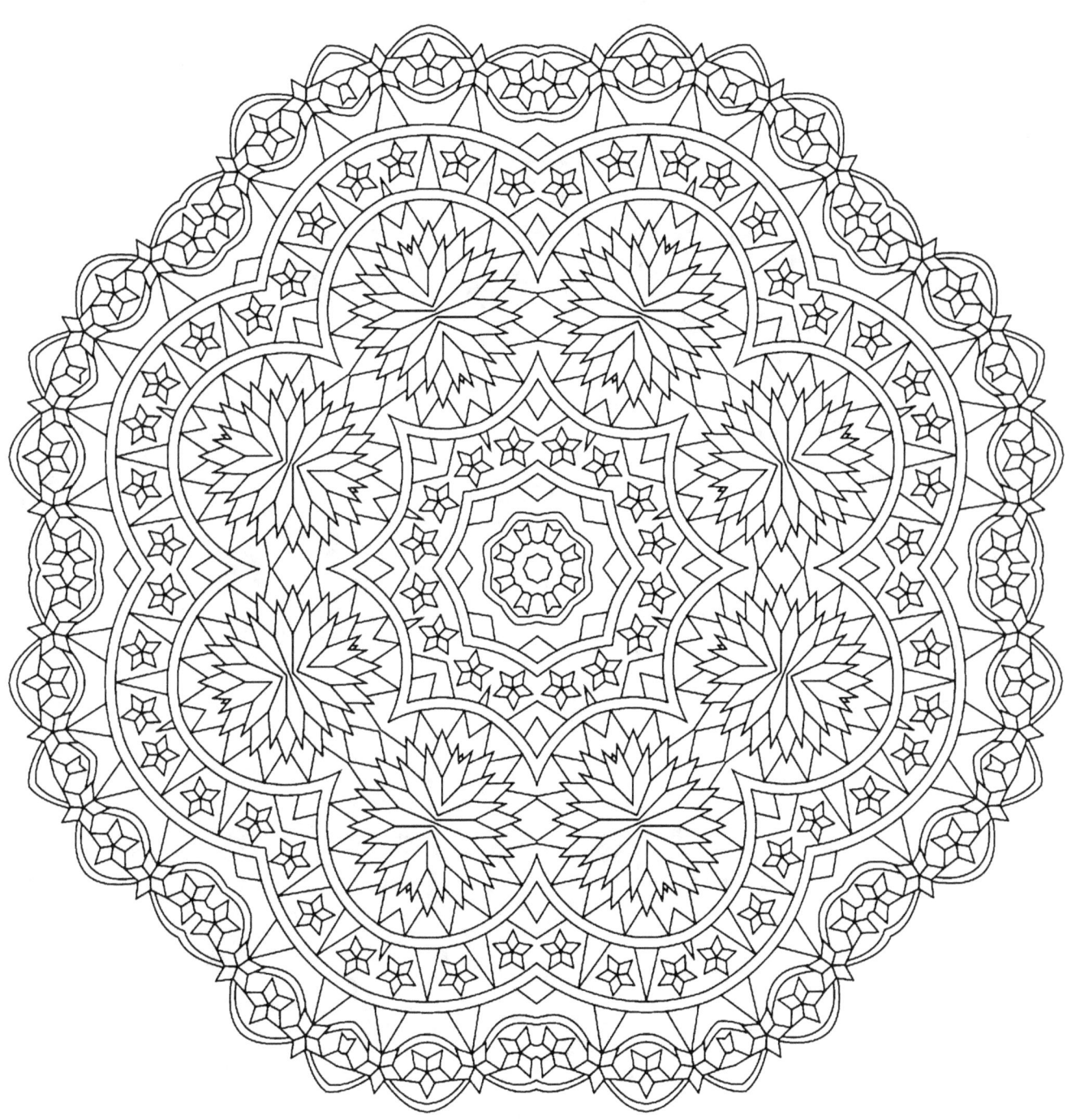

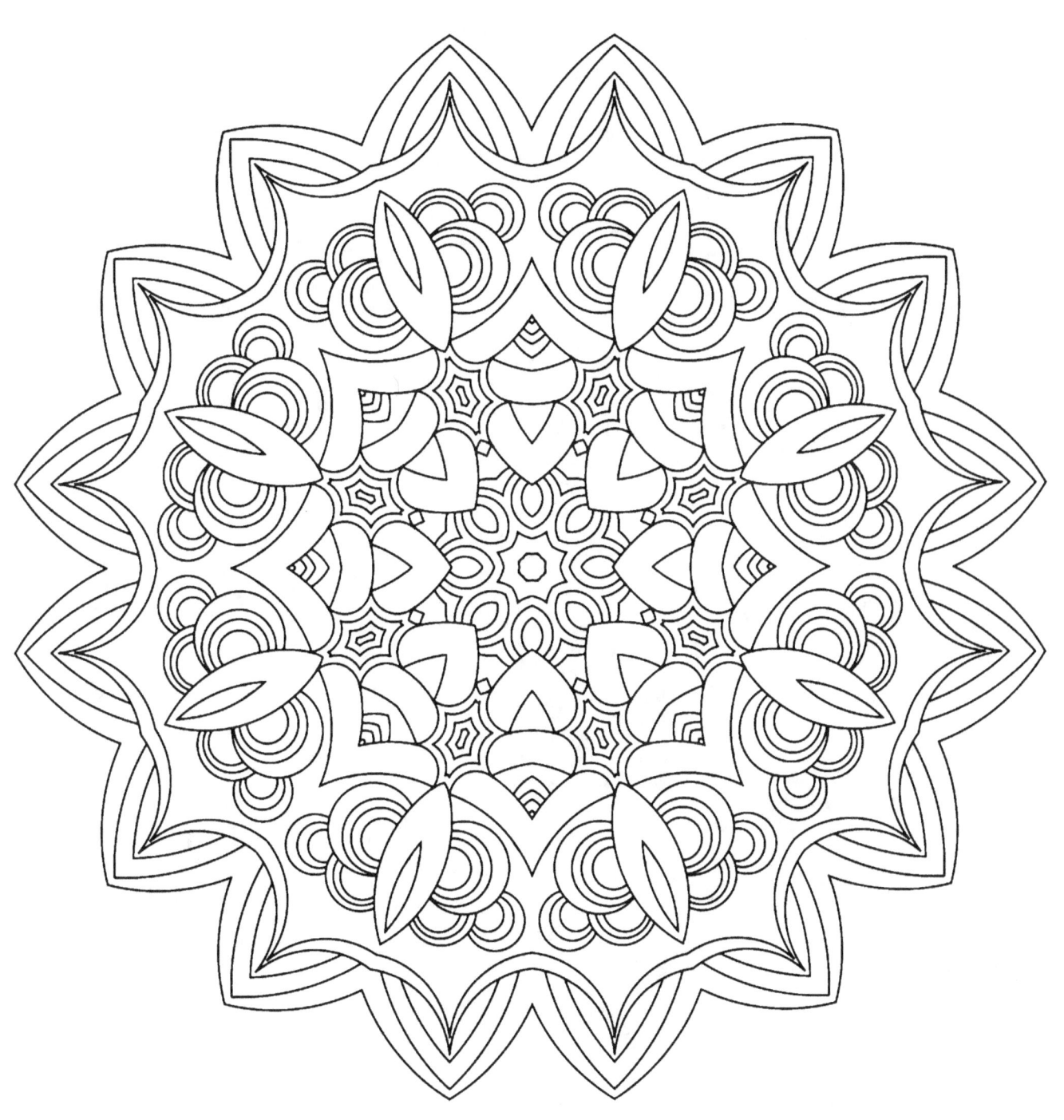

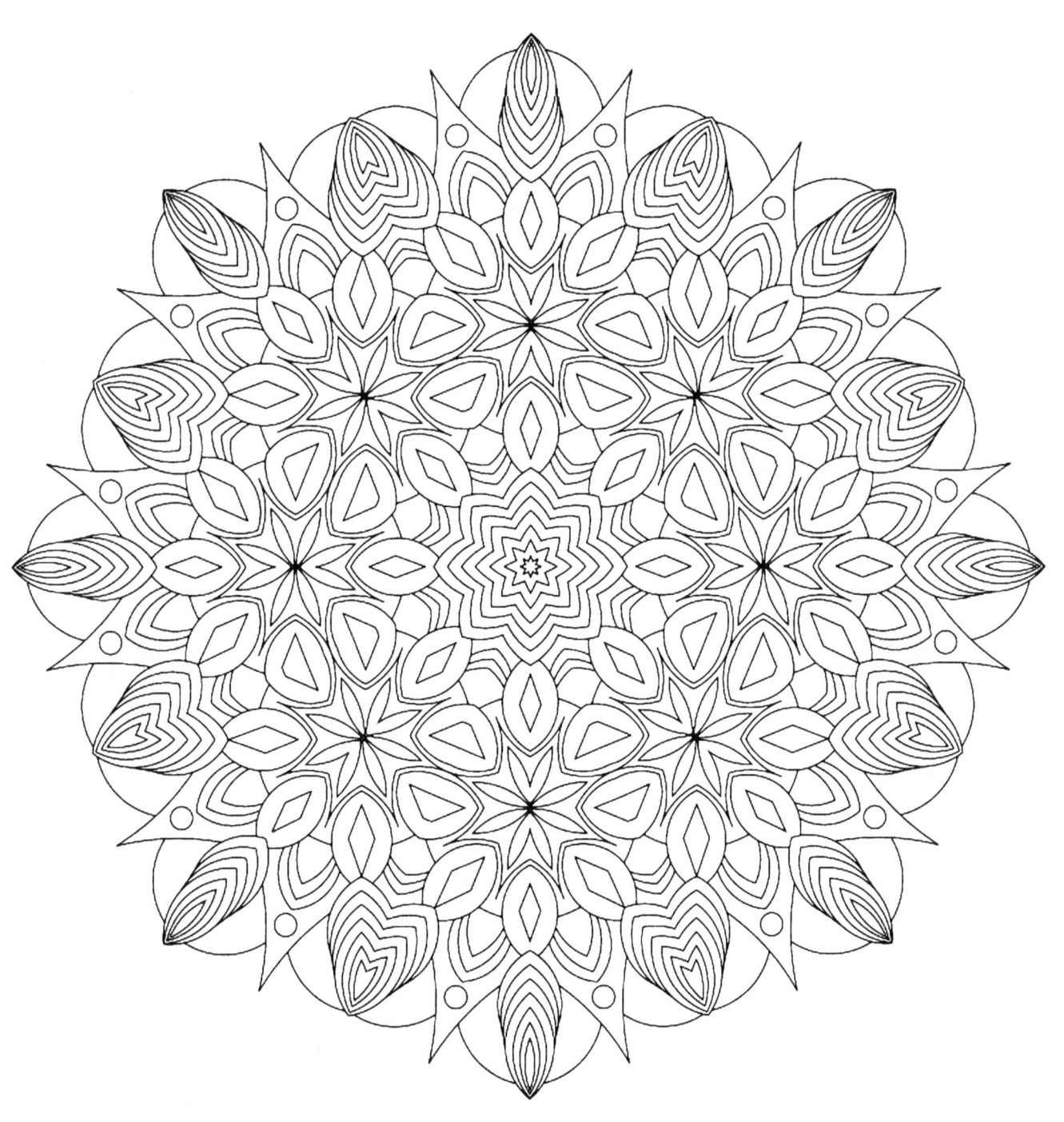

Blank Page

Remove and Insert Between
Pages if Using Wet Media

Blank Page

Remove and Insert Between
Pages if Using Wet Media